# Simple Machines

## Force, Motion, and Energy

## Expanding Science Skills Series

BY

JOHN B. BEAVER, PH.D., AND BARBARA R. SANDALL, ED.D.

CONSULTANTS: SCHYRLET CAMERON AND CAROLYN CRAIG

COPYRIGHT © 2010 Mark Twain Media, Inc.

ISBN 978-1-58037-523-8

Printing No. CD-404120

Visit us at www.carsondellosa.com

Mark Twain Media, Inc., Publishers
Distributed by Carson-Dellosa Publishing LLC

The purchase of this book entitles the buyer to reproduce the student pages for classroom use only. Other permissions may be obtained by writing Mark Twain Media, Inc., Publishers.

*All rights reserved. Printed in the United States of America.*

# Table of Contents

# Introduction

*Simple Machines: Force, Motion, and Energy* is one of the books in Mark Twain Media's new *Expanding Science Skills Series*. The easy-to-follow format of each book facilitates planning for the diverse learning styles and skill levels of middle-school students. The teacher information page provides a quick overview of the lesson to be taught. National science, mathematics, and technology standards, concepts, and science process skills are identified and listed, simplifying lesson preparation. Materials lists for Knowledge Builder activities are included where appropriate. Strategies presented in the lesson planner section provide the teacher with alternative methods of instruction: reading exercises for concept development, hands-on activities to strengthen understanding of concepts, and investigations for inquiry learning. The challenging activities in the extended-learning section provide opportunities for students who excel to expand their learning.

*Simple Machines: Force, Motion, and Energy* is written for classroom teachers, parents, and students. This book can be used as a full unit of study or as individual lessons to supplement existing textbooks or curriculum programs. This book can be used as an enhancement to what is being done in the classroom or as a tutorial at home. The procedures and content background are clearly explained in the student information pages and include activities and investigations that can be completed individually or in a group setting. Materials used in the activities are commonly found at home or in the science classroom.

The *Expanding Science Skills Series* is designed to provide students in grades 5 through 8 and beyond with many opportunities to acquire knowledge, learn skills, explore scientific phenomena, and develop attitudes important to becoming scientifically literate. Other books in the series include *Chemistry, Electricity and Magnetism, Geology, Meteorology, Light and Sound,* and *Astronomy*.

The books in this series support the No Child Left Behind (NCLB) Act. The series promotes student knowledge and understanding of science and mathematics concepts through the use of good scientific techniques. The content, activities, and investigations are designed to strengthen scientific literacy skills and are correlated to the National Science Education Standards (NSES), the National Council for Teachers of Mathematics Standards (NCTM), and the Standards for Technological Literacy (STL). Correlations to state, national, and Canadian provincial standards are available at www.carsondellosa.com.

# How to Use This Book

The format of *Simple Machines: Force, Motion, and Energy* is specifically designed to facilitate the planning and teaching of science. Our goal is to provide teachers with strategies and suggestions on how to successfully implement each lesson in the book. Units are divided into two parts: teacher information and student information.

## Teacher Information Page

Each unit begins with a Teacher Information page. The purpose is to provide a snapshot of the unit. It is intended to guide the teacher through the development and implementation of the lessons in the unit of study. The Teacher Information page includes:

- National Standards: The unit is correlated with the National Science Education Standards (NSES), the National Council of Teachers of Mathematics Standards (NCTM), and the Standards for Technological Literacy (STL). Pages 62–66 contain a complete list and description of the National Standards.
- Concepts/Naïve Concepts: The relevant science concepts and the commonly held student misconceptions are listed.
- Science Process Skills: The process skills associated with the unit are explained. Pages 67–70 contain a complete list and description of the Science Process Skills.
- Lesson Planner: The components of the lesson are described: directed reading, assessment, hands-on activities, materials lists of Knowledge Builder activities, and investigation.
- Extension: This activity provides opportunities for students who excel to expand their learning.
- Real World Application: The concept being taught is related to everyday life.

## Student Pages

The Student Information pages follow the Teacher Information page. The built-in flexibility of this section accommodates a diversity of learning styles and skill levels. The format allows the teacher to begin the lesson with basic concepts and vocabulary presented in reading exercises and expand to progressively more difficult hands-on activities found on the Knowledge Builder and Inquiry Investigation pages. The Student Information pages include:

1. Student Information: introduces the concepts and essential vocabulary for the lesson in a directed reading exercise.
2. Quick Check: evaluates student comprehension of the information in the directed reading exercise.
3. Knowledge Builder: strengthens student understanding of concepts with hands-on activities.
4. Inquiry Investigation: explores concepts introduced in the directed reading exercise through labs, models, and exploration activities.

**Safety Tip:** Adult supervision is recommended for all activities, especially those where chemicals, heat sources, electricity, or sharp or breakable objects are used. Safety goggles, gloves, hot pads, and other safety equipment should be used where appropriate.

# Unit 1: Historical Perspective
## Teacher Information

**Topic:** Many individuals have contributed to the science of force and motion as it relates to machines.

**Standards:**
>    **NSES** Unifying Concepts and Processes, (A), (B), (F), (G)
>    **STL** Technology and Society
>    See **National Standards** section (pages 62–66) for more information on each standard.

**Concepts:**
- Science and technology have advanced through contributions of many different people, in different cultures, at different times in history.
- Tracing the history of science can show how difficult it was for scientific innovations to break through the accepted ideas of their time to reach the conclusions we currently take for granted.

**Naïve Concepts:**
- All scientists wear lab coats.
- Scientists are totally absorbed in their research, oblivious to the world around them.
- Ideas and discoveries made by scientists from other cultures and civilizations before modern times are not relevant today.

**Science Process Skills:**

Students will be **collecting**, **recording**, and **interpreting information** while **developing the vocabulary to communicate** the results of their reading and research. Based on their findings, students will make an **inference** that many individuals have contributed to the traditions of the science of force and motion as it relates to machines.

**Lesson Planner:**
1. <u>Directed Reading</u>: Introduce the concepts and essential vocabulary relating to the history of the science of machines using the directed reading exercise found on the Student Information pages.
2. <u>Assessment</u>: Evaluate student comprehension of the information in the directed reading exercise using the quiz located on the Quick Check page.
3. <u>Concept Reinforcement</u>: Strengthen student understanding of concepts with the activities found on the Knowledge Builder page. **Materials Needed:** Activity #1—3 x 5-inch index cards, yarn, glue, and colored pencils; Activity #2—white paper, scissors

**Extension:** Students research the history of the catapult. They use the information to build their own catapults. They compete to see whose catapult can fling a marshmallow the farthest.

**Real World Application:** The Egyptians were able to move extremely heavy stones to build the pyramids with wedges, levers, and wheels. They would not have been able to move the stones without these machines.

# Unit 1: Historical Perspective
## Student Information

Simple machines are basic tools that help people do work easier and faster. The six simple machines are the lever, wheel and axle, pulley, inclined plane, wedge, and screw. Ancient people discovered these tools over time. Tools date back to 6000 B.C. when wedges like arrows and spears were used for hunting. In 3000 B.C., levers and ramps, a type of inclined plane, were used to move heavy loads. At the same time, wooden ships traveled the seas. In 2000 B.C., horse-drawn vehicles were used, and spoke wheels were invented. In 1500 B.C., pulleys were used by the Assyrians, and in 1000 B.C., woodworking lathes, cranes, and complex pulleys were used.

Archimedes (287–212 B.C.) discovered the Principle of Mechanical Advantage as it applied to levers and pulleys. This principle is the underlying foundation for our understanding of how simple machines work. He also invented the Archimedean Screw. The **Archimedean Screw** was a device invented to raise water. It consisted of a screw snugly fit into a cylindrical casing and was used in the Nile Valley for irrigation.

From A.D. 1 to A.D. 500, waterwheels that worked by using wheels and axles, Roman wood planes that were wedges, and Chinese cranks, which were another application of a wheel and axle, were all developed. The wheelbarrow, a second-class lever, was invented in China during this time.

Heron of Alexandria (A.D. 10–75) was an engineer who is considered to be the greatest experimenter of antiquity. One of his many contributions to the sciences was *Mechanics*. His work listed five devices (winch, lever, pulley, wedge, and screw) that could be used to move a load. It would be almost 1,400 years before scientists amended this list.

*Heron of Alexandria*

The wheel is often considered one of humankind's greatest inventions. Wheeled vehicles were first used in Mesopotamia in 3500 B.C. Levers, ramps, and wheels were used by the ancient Egyptians to build the pyramids, the Greeks to build their temples, and the Romans to build the Coliseum. All of these monuments were built using nothing but simple machines.

The ancient Romans used catapults, a third-class lever that works like a slingshot and is capable of launching heavy objects, to throw stones at their enemies. The catapult proved to be one of the most effective mechanisms used in warfare during this time.

People began studying the five simple machines during the Renaissance (1400s). In 1600, Galileo Galilei (1564–1642) wrote *On Mechanics*, which expanded the theory behind simple machines. He explained that simple machines do not create energy, they only transform it. Galileo identified the lever, wheel and axle, pulley, inclined plane, and screw as the five simple machines. He did not include Heron's winch or wedge. However, later scientists added the wedge back to the list.

*Galileo Galilei*

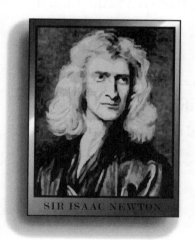

Sir Isaac Newton (1642–1727), is responsible for the Laws of Motion. In 1686, he presented his three Laws of Motion. They are necessary to understanding how work is done by simple machines. The **First Law**, also known as the Law of Inertia, states an object at rest stays at rest until acted upon by another force; it stays in motion in a straight line at a constant speed until acted upon by another force. The **Second Law**, also known as the Law of Acceleration, states that acceleration produced by a force on a body is directly proportional to the magnitude of the net force, is in the same direction as the force, and is inversely proportional to the mass of the body. Newton's **Third Law**, also known as the Law of Action and Reaction, states that for every action there is an equal and opposite reaction.

Between the eighteenth and nineteenth centuries, the **Industrial Revolution** began in Europe and spread to North America. It changed how goods were produced. Before the revolution, most people worked at producing items by hand using simple machines. Factories using power-driven compound machines quickly replaced the old method of handmade goods.

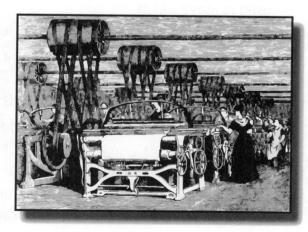

We still use simple machines today, by themselves and as part of more complex machines.

Name: _____ Date: _____

# Quick Check

## Matching

_____ 1.   catapult

_____ 2.   Archimedian screw

_____ 3.   Law of Acceleration

_____ 4.   Law of Inertia

_____ 5.   Law of Action and Reaction

a.   Newton's First Law of Motion

b.   Newton's Second Law of Motion

c.   Newton's Third Law of Motion

d.   a device invented to raise water

e.   a machine capable of launching heavy objects

## Fill in the Blanks

6.   Between the eighteenth and nineteenth centuries, the _____ _____ began in Europe and spread to North America.

7.   _____ (287–212 B.C.) discovered the laws of levers and pulleys.

8.   The Third Law of Motion states that for every _____ there is an equal and opposite _____.

9.   The Second Law of Motion states that acceleration produced by a _____ on a body is directly proportional to the magnitude of the _____ _____, is in the same direction as the force, and is inversely proportional to the mass of the body.

10.  The First Law of Motion states an object at rest stays at rest until acted upon by another force; it stays in _____ in a straight line at a _____ speed until acted upon by another force.

## Multiple Choice

11.  His work, *Mechanics*, listed five devices (winch, lever, pulley, wedge, and screw) that could be used to move a load.

    a.   Archimedes

    c.   Galileo Galilei

    b.   Heron of Alexandria

    d.   Sir Isaac Newton

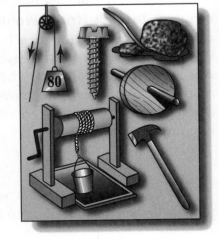

12.  Where were wheeled vehicles first used?

    a.   Egypt

    c.   Mesopotamia

    b.   Rome

    d.   China

13.  He is the scientist responsible for the three Laws of Motion.

    a.   Archimedes

    c.   Sir Isaac Newton

    b.   Galileo Galilei

    d.   Heron of Alexandria

Name: _____ Date: _____

# Knowledge Builder

## Activity #1: String Time Line

**Directions:** Research the history of tools and simple machines. Using the information and the Student Information pages, create a time line that shows the use of simple machines through history. Cut a piece of yarn 2 meters long. Place the date the machine was used on a 3 x 5-inch index card. On the back of the index card, draw the machine and write one sentence describing the machine and its uses. Punch a hole in the top of the card and tie it to your yarn time line in the appropriate place. Do this with five other simple machines. Be sure to put the cards in chronological order and leave enough string on both ends to allow you to tie or tack the time line to display it.

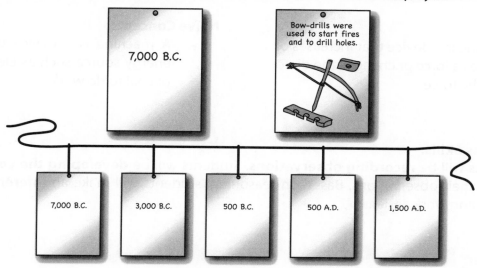

## Activity #2: Scientists Tab Book

**Directions:** Research the four scientists found on the Student Information pages. Using your information, create a graphic organizer to display your research. Fold a white sheet of paper in half making a hotdog bun. Now, fold the sheet of paper into four equal parts. Unfold the paper and cut up the three fold lines, making four tabs. Label each tab with the name of a scientist. Under each appropriate tab, write information about the scientist and their contribution to the science of machines.

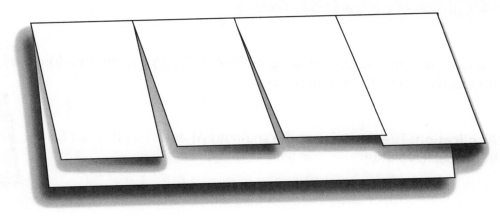

# Unit 2: Machines
## Teacher Information

**Topic:** A machine is any device that makes doing work easier.

**Standards:**
**NSES** Unifying Concepts and Processes, (A), (B), (E), (F), (G)
**NCTM** Geometry and Measurement
**STL** Technology and Society
See **National Standards** section (pages 62–66) for more information on each standard.

**Concepts:**
- A machine is a device that increases or decreases a force or changes the direction of the force.

**Naïve Concepts:**
- A machine is a device that uses an energy source such as electricity, gas, or coal to do work.

**Science Process Skills:**
Students will be **recording observations**. Students will be **developing the vocabulary to communicate** their observations. Based on reasoning, students will make an **inference** that machines make doing work easier.

**Lesson Planner:**
1. Directed Reading: Introduce the concepts and essential vocabulary relating to machines using the directed reading exercise found on the Student Information page.

2. Assessment: Evaluate student comprehension of the information in the directed reading exercise using the quiz located on the Quick Check page.

3. Concept Reinforcement: Strengthen student understanding of concepts with the activities found on the Knowledge Builder page. **Materials Needed:** Activity #1—white paper, scissors, pencils; Activity #2—hand-cranked can opener

**Extension:** Students research Rube Goldberg machines. Using the information, they construct a Rube Goldberg machine to perform a simple task.

**Real World Application:** The invention of the spinning wheel is given credit for starting the Industrial Revolution.

# Unit 2: Machines
## Student Information

Machines have changed the way in which we do work. A **machine** is any device that makes doing work easier. They reduce the force you have to apply to do the work.

Advantages of using a machine:
- Makes doing work easier by reducing the force exerted
- Changes the distance over which the force is exerted
- Changes the direction of the force

Some of the machines we use everyday are **simple machines**. They have few or no moving parts to them. These machines help us to move objects closer, apart, or to raise them to different levels by increasing the force or changing the direction of the force.

Simple machines are designed to do specific jobs.
- A **lever** is a rigid bar that is free to rotate about a point called a fulcrum.
- The **pulley** is a wheel that turns readily on an axle. The axle is usually mounted on a frame.
- The **wheel and axle** is a wheel rigidly fixed to an axle.
- The **inclined plane** is a device that allows us to increase the height of an object without lifting it vertically.
- The **wedge** is a double inclined plane.
- The **screw** is an inclined plane wound around a cylinder.

Simple machines may be classified into two groups: levers and inclined planes. Levers include the lever, the pulley, and the wheel and axle. Inclined planes include the inclined plane, the wedge, and the screw.

A **compound machine** or complex machine has two or more simple machines working together to make work easier. Most machines are compound machines. Compound machines can do more difficult jobs than simple machines alone. Their mechanical advantage is far greater, too. Examples of compound machines are the wheelbarrow, scissors, can opener, bicycle, and automobile.

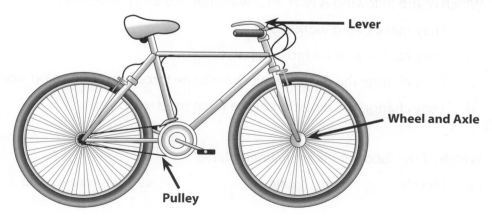

# Quick Check

## Matching

_____ 1.  wheel and axle

_____ 2.  screw

_____ 3.  wedge

_____ 4.  lever

_____ 5.  pulley

a.  a double inclined plane

b.  a wheel rigidly fixed to an axle

c.  a rigid bar that is free to rotate about a point called a fulcrum

d.  a wheel that turns readily on an axle

e.  an inclined plane wound around a cylinder

## Fill in the Blanks

6.  Simple machines may be classified into two groups: _____ and
    _____ _____.

7.  A _____ is any device that makes doing work easier.

8.  _____ _____ can do more difficult jobs than simple machines alone.

9.  A compound machine or _____ machine has two or more simple machines working together to make work easier.

10. The _____ _____ is a device that allows us to increase the height of an object without lifting it vertically.

## Multiple Choice

11. Which of the following is NOT a simple machine?

    a.  screw           b.  wedge           c.  pulley           d.  scissors

12. Which of the following is NOT an advantage of using a machine?

    a.  They make doing work easier.

    b.  They have few or no moving parts.

    c.  They change the distance over which the force is exerted to do work.

    d.  They change the direction of the force used to do work.

13. Which of the following is an inclined plane?

    a.  bicycle         b.  pulley          c.  wheel and axle          d.  screw

Name: _____   Date: _____

# Knowledge Builder

## Activity #1: Simple Machine Guide

**Directions:** Fold a sheet of white, unlined paper in half like a hotdog bun. Next fold the paper in thirds and then in sixths. Unfold the paper. You now have a hot-dog bun folded in 6 equal parts. Form 6 tabs by cutting along the folds on one side of the paper. Label each tab with the name of one of the six simple machines. Write a definition and important information under each appropriate tab. Use the foldable to help you study and remember simple machines.

## Activity #2: Compound Machines

**Directions:** Carefully examine a hand-cranked can opener. List all the simple machines found in the compound machine. In the data table below, describe how the simple machines identified in the can opener work together to open the can. Now, find four other compound machines around your home. Carefully examine each compound machine. List all the simple machines found in each compound machine. In the data table below, describe how the simple machines identified in each compound machine work together to perform a task.

| Compound Machine | Simple Machines in the Compound Machine |
|---|---|
| Hand-cranked can opener | |
| | |
| | |
| | |
| | |

# Unit 3: Force and Motion
## Teacher Information

**Topic:** Work is the force needed to move an object through a distance.

**Standards:**
**NSES** Unifying Concepts and Processes, (A), (B), (E), (F), (G)
**NCTM** Number and Operations and Algebra
**STL** Technology and Society
See **National Standards** section (pages 62–66) for more information on each standard.

**Concepts:**
- Work is the product of the effort force multiplied by the distance through which the object is moved.

**Naïve Concepts:**
- Work is the product of a person performing a mental or physical activity for a purpose or out of necessity.

**Science Process Skills:**

Students will **develop vocabulary** relating to work. Students will make an **inference** that work is the force needed to move an object through a distance.

**Lesson Planner:**

1. <u>Directed Reading</u>: Introduce the concepts and essential vocabulary relating to work using the directed reading exercise found on the Student Information page.

2. <u>Assessment</u>: Evaluate student comprehension of the information in the directed reading exercise using the quiz located on the Quick Check page.

3. <u>Concept Reinforcement</u>: Strengthen student understanding of concepts with the activities found on the Knowledge Builder page. **Materials Needed:** Activity #1—dish soap

**Extension:** Students research Newton's Laws of Motion. They choose a law and design an experiment that proves the law.

**Real World Application:** Archimedes' Screw was invented to move water. Today, it is frequently found moving corn and wheat in grain elevators.

# Unit 3: Force and Motion
## Student Information

Work, in everyday language, has many meanings. It might mean that we are exerting muscular effort, or it may simply refer to our daily duties related to job or school. In science, the word *work* has a particular meaning. Work is done when a force acts on a body and moves it. In physical science, **work** is the force needed to move an object though a distance. Pushing, pulling, and lifting are common forms of work. You do work when you raise a 20-kilogram load to your shoulder or when you carry the load up a flight of stairs or push it across the floor.

Two factors must be considered then when measuring work: (1) the force applied and (2) the distance through which the force acts. In work, distance is the change of position of an object. The formula for calculating work is: **W = F x d** (W = work, F = Force, and d = distance).

Simple machines offer mechanical advantage. **Mechanical advantage** compares the force produced by a machine with the force applied to the machine. It can be found by dividing the force of resistance by the force of the effort. **Mechanical Advantage = Force of Resistance (load)/Force of Effort.**

This formula calculates an ideal mechanical advantage and does not take into consideration the friction involved. **Friction** is a force that resists motion. It can reduce the amount of work that can be done with a given force. Another force involved with machines is **inertia**, the resistance of an object to change its motion.

It is necessary to understand motion when studying how work is done by machines. **Motion** is the act of moving from one place to another. Isaac Newton is the English scientist who stated the three Laws of Motion in 1687. The laws were named after him. **Newton's Laws of Motion** explain the relationship between force and motion.

- The **First Law** (Law of Inertia) states an object at rest stays at rest until acted upon by another force; it stays in motion in a straight line at a constant speed until acted upon by another force. For example, if a ball is not moving, it will stay that way until some force makes it move.
- The **Second Law** (Law of Acceleration) states that acceleration produced by a force on a body is directly proportional to the magnitude of the net force, is in the same direction as the force, and is inversely proportional to the mass of the body. For example, if two bike riders pedal with the same force, the rider moving less mass accelerates faster.
- The **Third Law** (Law of Action and Reaction) states that for every action there is an equal and opposite reaction. For example, a boy jumps on a trampoline. The action force is the boy pushing down on the trampoline. The reaction force is the trampoline pushing up on the boy.

**Energy** is the ability to do work. **Mechanical energy** is the energy an object has because of its motion or position. There are two kinds of mechanical energy: kinetic and potential. **Kinetic energy** is the energy an object has because it is moving. **Potential energy** is the energy an object has when it is at rest (stored energy) and depends on the object's position or shape.

Name: _____    Date: _____

# Quick Check

## Matching

_____ 1.  motion

_____ 2.  friction

_____ 3.  energy

_____ 4.  work

_____ 5.  potential energy

a.  stored energy

b.  force needed to move an object though a distance

c.  ability to do work

d.  act of moving from one place to another

e.  a force that resists motion

## Fill in the Blanks

6.  _____ _____ compares the force produced by a machine with the force applied to the machine.

7.  _____ _____ is the energy an object has because of its motion or position.

8.  Newton's Laws of Motion explain the relationship between _____ and _____.

9.  _____ _____ is the energy an object has because it is moving.

10.  Two factors must be considered when measuring work: (1) the _____ applied and (2) the _____ through which the force acts.

## Multiple Choice

11.  This law states that for every action there is an equal and opposite reaction.

   a.  Third Law

   c.  Second Law

   b.  First Law

   d.  Law of Inertia

12.  This law states that acceleration produced by a force on a body is directly proportional to the magnitude of the net force, is in the same direction as the force, and is inversely proportional to the mass of the body.

   a.  First Law

   c.  Law of Action and Reaction

   b.  Third Law

   d.  Second Law

13.  This law states an object at rest stays at rest until acted upon by another force; it stays in motion in a straight line at a constant speed until acted upon by another force.

   a.  Law of Acceleration

   c.  Third Law

   b.  First Law

   d.  Second Law

Name: _____          Date: _____

# Knowledge Builder

## Activity #1: Friction

**Directions:** Friction is a force that slows down and stops moving objects. It is a resistance to motion. Friction is created whenever objects rub against each other. Friction can produce heat and wear objects down.

1.  Rub the palms of your hands together quickly for 30 seconds. What did you feel? _____
    _____

2.  Put a few drops of liquid dishwashing soap on your hands. Rub your hands together quickly for 30 seconds. Did your hands feel the same as they did without the soap? _____
    Why? _____

Conclusions

1.  How did using dishwashing soap help reduce the friction between your hands? _____
    _____

2.  How does oil affect a machine? _____
    _____

## Activity #2: Measuring Work

**Directions:** Refer to the definition for work below and complete the following exercise. First, place a check on the blanks below each statement to determine if the statement fulfills the requirements for the definition of work. Then, place a (+) on the blank if work is done. Place a (-) on the blank if no work is performed.

Definition for work: **A force is applied to an object, and the object moves as a result of the force.**

_____ 1.  You push a desk across the room.
            _____ A force was applied.          _____ The object moves as a result of a force.

_____ 2.  You try to move a large boulder by pushing it. After ten minutes of hard pushing, you find the boulder has not moved.
            _____ A force was applied.          _____ The object moves as a result of a force.

_____ 3.  You stand for 15 minutes holding a box of books for a friend.
            _____ A force was applied.          _____ The object moves as a result of a force.

_____ 4.  You ride your bike to school.
            _____ A force was applied.          _____ The object moves as a result of a force.

# Unit 4: Levers
## Teacher Information

**Topic:** There are three classes of levers.

**Standards:**
   **NSES** Unifying Concepts and Processes, (A), (B), (E), (F)
   **NCTM** Measurement and Data Analysis and Probability
   **STL** Technology and Society
   See **National Standards** section (pages 62–66) for more information on each standard.

**Concepts:**
- Two factors must be considered when measuring work: (1) the force applied and (2) the distance through which the force acts.
- Mechanical advantage compares the force produced by a machine with the force applied to the machine.

**Naïve Concepts:**
- Force is a property of an object.
- A machine is a device that uses an energy source such as electricity, gas, or coal to do work.

**Science Process Skills:**
Students will make **observations** about the relative force needed to lift an object with different classes of levers and make **inferences** about the mechanical advantage and the direction, force, and distance through which a force acts; **classify** various examples of levers into one of the three lever classes; **measure** the relative effort needed to move a resistance; **communicate** with others and **make predictions**; **describe** what will happen as they **manipulate materials** to **create models**; learn new words or unique uses of common words in relation to a given topic; **draw general conclusions** from particular details; **record**, **interpret**, and **analyze** data gathered from **experiments** to **make decisions**.

**Lesson Planner:**
1. Directed Reading: Introduce the concepts and essential vocabulary relating to levers using the directed reading exercise found on the Student Information pages.
2. Assessment: Evaluate student comprehension of the information in the directed reading exercise using the quiz located on the Quick Check page.
3. Concept Reinforcement: Strengthen student understanding of concepts with the activities found on the Knowledge Builder pages. **Materials Needed:** Activity #1, #2, #3, and #4—10 pennies or washers, meter stick, string, tape, 2 rubber bands (1 cm wide), paper clip, 2 small paper cups with a string attached to the top of each
4. Inquiry Investigation: Construct a cantilever. Divide the class into teams. Instruct each team to complete the Inquiry Investigation pages.

**Extension:** Students research how the ancient Egyptians used levers to build the pyramids.

**Real World Application:** Levers have been used since prehistoric times to reduce the amount of force needed to do work. For example, using a pry bar to move a heavy rock is much easier than trying to lift the rock with your hands.

# Unit 4: Levers
## Student Information

The simplest machine is a lever. A **lever** is a bar that can turn on a fixed point, the **fulcrum**. A lever can be used to multiply the force or change the direction of the force. A lever has a **resistance or load** (the object being moved), a **fulcrum or pivot point** for the bar, and a **force** (any push or pull on an object) to move the object. As shown in the diagrams, the effort force and effort movement are in the same direction. The resistance force is in the direction of gravity, and the resistance motion is in the opposite direction. The resistance on the machine may be due to the force of gravity, friction, and inertia. In order to simplify the discussion, the **resistance force** referred to in this book is the force of gravity.

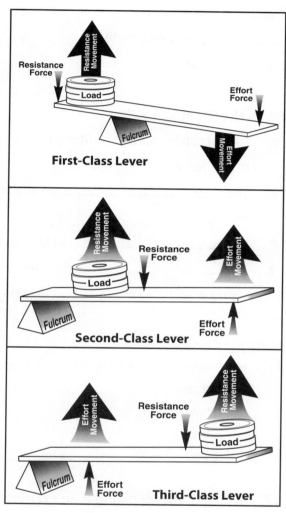

There are three classes of levers. Using a **first-class lever**, the force changes directions. The load is on one side of the fulcrum, and the forces are on the other side of the lever. When the force pushes down on one end, the load (resistance) moves up. An example of this would be using a crowbar to pry the lid off a box.

In a **second-class lever**, the load is placed between the force and the fulcrum. The direction of the force stays the same as the load. The force on the load is increased; however, the load will not move as far. An example of this is a wheelbarrow.

The **third-class lever** is similar to the first-class lever with the fulcrum at one end and the load on the other end. However, a third-class lever has the force applied between the fulcrum and the load. The effort force and the load are moving in the same direction. An example of this type of lever is your elbow and your lower arm. The fulcrum is your elbow, and the load is your hand. The force is applied in the middle by your biceps muscles.

A **cantilever** is an example of a lever that consists of an arm supported at only one end. The mass of the arm and the load it carries must be counterbalanced at the fulcrum. Railroad crossing arms and stoplight supports are examples of cantilevers.

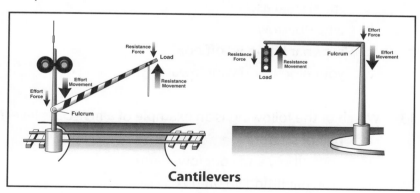

Cantilevers

Name: _____    Date: _____

# Quick Check

## Matching

_____ 1. resistance force
_____ 2. fulcrum
_____ 3. lever
_____ 4. resistance or load
_____ 5. force

a. any push or pull on an object
b. a bar that can turn on a fixed point
c. force of gravity
d. pivot point
e. the object being moved

## Fill in the Blanks

6. A lever can be used to multiply the _____ or change the _____ of the force.

7. The _____ on the machine may be due to the force of gravity, friction, and inertia.

8. In a _____- class lever, the load is placed between the force and the fulcrum.

9. A _____-class lever has the force applied between the fulcrum and the load.

10. Using a _____-class lever, the force changes directions.

## Multiple Choice

11. How many classes of levers are there?
    a. three
    b. two
    c. four
    d. six

12. Which of the following is an example of a second-class lever?
    a. spiral staircase
    b. wheelbarrow
    c. crowbar lifting lid off box
    d. your elbow and your lower arm

13. Which of the following is an example of a first-class lever?
    a. pair of scissors
    b. your elbow and your lower arm
    c. crowbar lifting lid off box
    d. wheelbarrow

Name: _____     Date: _____

# Knowledge Builder

## Activity #1: First-Class Levers

**Directions:**

<u>Part A</u>: Construct a first-class lever as shown. Tie a string at the 50-cm mark of the meter stick. Attach the string to a table to suspend the meter stick. The string will become the fulcrum. Attach a cup to the 2-cm mark and a cup to the 98-cm mark. Move the fulcrum so the meter stick (lever arm) is balanced. Record the location of the fulcrum.

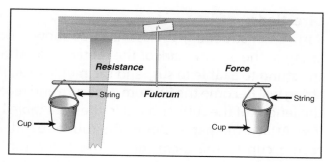

| Location cup 1 (cm) | Location cup 2 (cm) | Location of Fulcrum (cm) |
|---|---|---|
| 2 cm | 98 cm | |

<u>Part B</u>: Use the same setup as Part A above. Add 1 penny to one cup and 2 pennies to the other cup. Move the fulcrum so the lever arm balances again. Record the location of the fulcrum. Repeat the procedure 2 more times by adding 1 penny to one cup and 5 pennies to the other cup and then adding 1 penny to one cup and 10 pennies to the other cup. Record the location of the fulcrum each time.

| Location Cup 1 (cm) | Cup 1 # of Pennies | Location Cup 2 (cm) | Cup 2 # of Pennies | Location of Fulcrum (cm) |
|---|---|---|---|---|
| 2 cm | 1 | 98 cm | 2 | |
| | | | | |
| | | | | |

Observation

1. What happened to the distance between the fulcrum and the resistance as more pennies were added to the resistance in one cup? _____

   _____

2. In what direction is the force being applied? _____

   _____

3. In what direction is the resistance moving? _____

   _____

Conclusion

What is the advantage of using a first-class lever? _____

_____

_____

Name: _____     Date: _____

# Knowledge Builder

## Activity #2: First-Class Levers

**Directions:**

<u>Part A</u>: Construct a first-class lever as shown. Tie a string at the 50-cm mark of the meter stick. Attach the string to a table to suspend the meter stick. The string will become the fulcrum. Measure and record the length of the rubber band in the data table below. Attach the paper clip to the rubber band. Attach a cup to the 2-cm mark. Attach the rubber

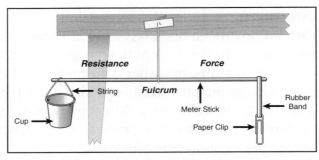

band to the other end of the meter stick at the 98-cm mark. Pull on the rubber band so the lever is level again. Measure and record the length of the rubber band.

<u>Part B</u>: Use the same setup as Part A above. Add 10 pennies to the cup. Pull on the rubber band attached to the end of the meter stick so the lever arm balances. Record the location of the fulcrum and the amount of force needed to balance the lever. Move the fulcrum string to the 40-cm mark. Pull on the rubber band so the lever arm balances again. Record the location of the fulcrum and the force needed to lift the resistance. Repeat the procedure 2 more times by moving the fulcrum to the 30-cm mark and then the 20-cm mark. Record the location of the fulcrum and the force needed to lift the resistance each time.

| Load | Location of Fulcrum (cm) | Length of Rubber Band (cm) |
|---|---|---|
| No load | 50 cm | |
| Cup | 50 cm | |
| Cup and 10 Pennies | | |
| Cup and 10 Pennies | | |
| Cup and 10 Pennies | | |
| Cup and 10 Pennies | | |

Observation

1. What happened to the length of the rubber band (effort force) as the fulcrum was moved closer to the cup (load)? _____

2. In what direction is the force being applied? _____

3. In what direction is the resistance moving? _____

Conclusion

Why would you use a first-class lever? _____

_____

_____

Name: _____     Date: _____

# Knowledge Builder

## Activity #3: Second-Class Levers

**Directions:**

Part A: Construct a second-class lever as shown. Tie a string at the 2-cm mark of the meter stick. Attach the string to a table to suspend the meter stick. The string will become the fulcrum. Slide a stringed cup on the meter stick at the 70-cm mark. Put a rubber band on the free end of the meter stick. Using the paper clip, attach the rubber band to the table. Measure the length of the rubber band in centimeters. Record the measurement in the data table. Place 10 pennies in the cup. Measure and record the length of the rubber band.

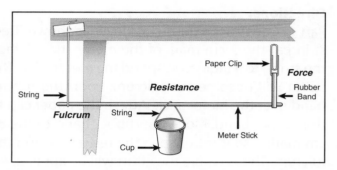

Part B: Use the same setup as Part A above. Slide the resistance (cup and 10 pennies) to the 50-cm mark. Record the location of the fulcrum in the data table below. Measure and record the length of the rubber band in centimeters. Repeat the procedure 2 more times by moving the resistance to the 30-cm mark and then the 10-cm mark.

| Load | Location of Fulcrum (cm) | Length of Rubber Band (cm) |
|---|---|---|
| Cup | 70 cm | |
| Cup and 10 Pennies | 70 cm | |
| Cup and 10 Pennies | | |
| Cup and 10 Pennies | | |
| Cup and 10 Pennies | | |

Observation

1.  What happened to the force needed to lift the resistance as the distance between the resistance and the fulcrum decreased? _____

    _____

2.  In what direction is the force being applied? _____

    _____

3.  In what direction is the resistance moving? _____

    _____

Conclusion

What will you gain from using a second-class lever? _____

_____

_____

Name: _____    Date: _____

# Knowledge Builder

## Activity #4: Third-Class Levers

**Directions:**

Part A: Construct a third-class lever as shown. Tie a string at the 2-cm mark of the meter stick. Attach the string to a table to suspend the meter stick. The string will become the fulcrum. Loop the rubber band over the meter stick. Attach the paper clip to the rubber band. Move the rubber band to the 80 cm marker so it is between the resistance and the fulcrum. This is where the effort will be applied. At-

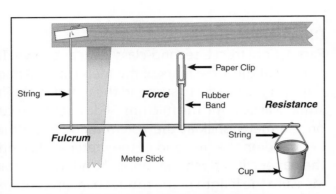

tach the cup at the 98-cm marker. This is the resistance. Lift the lever until it is level by pulling up on the paper clip on the rubber band. Measure the length of the rubber band in centimeters and record in the data table below. Put 10 pennies into the cup. Measure and record the length of the rubber band.

Part B: Use the same setup as Part A above. Attach the effort (rubber band) to the meter stick at the 50-cm mark so it is between the resistance (cup and 10 pennies) and the fulcrum (string). Record the force needed to lift the resistance. Attach the effort (rubber band) to the meter stick at the 20-cm mark so it is between the resistance (cup and 10 pennies) and the fulcrum (string). Record the force needed to lift the resistance.

| Load (# of Pennies) | Location of Rubber Band (cm) | Length of Rubber Band (cm) |
|---|---|---|
| 0 | 80 cm | |
| 10 | 80 cm | |
| 10 | | |
| 10 | | |

Observation

1.  What happened to the force needed to lift the resistance as the distance between the resistance and the fulcrum decreased? _____

    _____

2.  In what direction is the force being applied? _____

    _____

3.  In what direction is the resistance moving? _____

    _____

Conclusions _____

_____

_____

Name: _____     Date: _____

# Inquiry Investigation: Cantilevers

**Concept:**
- A cantilever is a type of lever that consists of an arm supported at one end (fulcrum). The mass of the arm and the load it carries must be counterbalanced at the fulcrum.

**Purpose:** Construct a cantilever.

**Procedure:** Carry out the investigation. This includes gathering the materials, following the step-by-step directions, and recording the data.

**Materials:**

| | | |
|---|---|---|
| 30 skewers | 1 penny | 1 small paper cup with 10-cm string attached |
| 30 cm masking tape | clay | 5 large washers |
| 1/2 paper egg carton | 4 craft sticks | |

**Prediction:** Based on the information gained from the first four lever activities, make a prediction of the longest arm that you could make and lift the load and where you would place the load, fulcrum, and resistance.

_____

_____

**Procedure:** Use any or all of the materials to construct a cantilever to meet the following criteria.

Step 1:     Make a free-standing cantilever that can hold the load of one penny.

Step 2:     Make the longest arm from the fulcrum to the load.

Step 3:     The height of the load from the table must be a minimum of 10 cm (measure from the bottom of the cup to the table top).

Step 4:     Attach the arm of the cantilever on the top of the tower.

Step 5:     Test different lengths of the arm. Record the length and results of each test in the data table below. You may need to make the drawing of each setup on your own paper.

| Trial # | Length of Arm (cm) | Drawing | Attempt Successful |
|---|---|---|---|
| | | | |
| | | | |
| | | | |
| | | | |

**Conclusion:**

What class of lever does your construction represent? Explain. _____

_____

_____

# Unit 5: Wheels and Axles
## Teacher Information

**Topic:** A wheel and axle is a wheel or crank rigidly attached to an axle.

**Standards:**
   **NSES** Unifying Concepts and Processes, (A), (B), (E), (F), (G)
   **NCTM** Geometry, Measurement, and Data Analysis and Probability
   **STL** Technology and Society
   See **National Standards** section (pages 62–66) for more information on each standard.

**Concepts:**
- Two factors must be considered when measuring work: (1) the force applied and (2) the distance through which the force acts.
- Mechanical advantage compares the force produced by a machine with the force applied to the machine.

**Naïve Concepts:**
- Force is a property of an object.
- A machine is a device that uses an energy source such as electricity, gas, or coal to do work.

**Science Process Skills:**
Students will **make observations** about the operation of a winch and the number of turns a string makes as it winds around a cylinder (drinking straw) as a crank is turned and **inferences** about the mechanical advantage and other uses for such a device; **infer** about the relationship of the wheel and axle to the lever; **apply knowledge** to the identification of examples of the wheel and axle in compound machines; **measure** the relative effort needed to move or lift a load or resistance; **collect and record data**; **identify** and **control variables**; **predict**; **interpret data**; and **apply the information** to examples outside the classroom.

**Lesson Planner:**
1. Directed Reading: Introduce the concepts and essential vocabulary relating to the wheel and axle using the directed reading exercise found on the Student Information page.
2. Assessment: Evaluate student comprehension of the information in the directed reading exercise using the quiz located on the Quick Check page.
3. Concept Reinforcement: Strengthen student understanding of concepts with the activity found on the Knowledge Builder page. **Materials Needed:** 3 paper clips, piece of string, steel or aluminum can, washers, 2 flexible drinking straws, masking tape, small cup

**Extension:** Students research the evolution of the wheel and its importance to humankind.

**Real World Application:** Almost every machine built since the beginning of the Industrial Revolution involves the wheel.

# Unit 5: Wheels and Axles
## Student Information

A **wheel and axle** is a wheel or crank rigidly attached to an axle. Examples of a wheel and axle include a playground merry-go-round, a screwdriver, a hand drill, a wrench, a faucet, and a steering wheel.

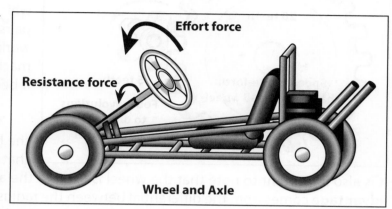

Wheel and Axle

The wheel and axle is another form of a lever. The bar is changed into a circle moving around a fulcrum. In the example pictured here, the steering wheel (wheel) is rigidly attached to the steering wheel column (axle). The radius of the steering wheel represents one lever and the radius of the steering wheel column represents a second lever. Hence, we have two wheels of unequal diameter, fastened so they turn together. In the steering wheel assembly, the effort force is applied to the steering wheel, and the steering wheel column represents the resistance force. Ideal mechanical advantage is equal to the diameter of the wheel (D) divided by the diameter of the axle (d). **IMA = D/d.**

A **winch system** is an example of a wheel and axle. The wheel portion of the system is represented by a crank, and the axle is represented by the cylinder-shaped body. The relative size of the crank or handle in a winch system will determine the mechanical advantage. A wishing well is an example of a device that uses a winch to draw water.

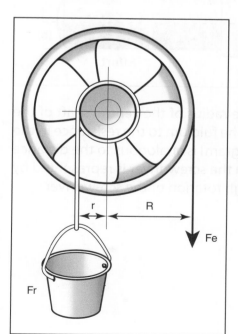

In the diagram at left, we have two wheels of unequal diameter, fastened so they turn together about the same axis. In one revolution, the effort force **(Fe)** moves a distance equal to the circumference **(C)** of the wheel. At the same time, the resistance force **(Fr)** will travel a distance equal to the circumference **(c)** of the axle. The **Ideal Mechanical Advantage** or **IMA = C/c or D/d or R/r**. **D** equals diameter, and **r** equals radius. Hence, if the radius of the wheel is 8 cm, and the radius of the axle is 2 cm, then the IMA = 4.

**r** = radius of the axle
**R** = radius of the wheel
**Fe** = Force of the effort
**Fr** = Force of the resistance

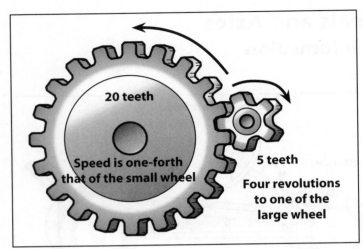

20 teeth

Speed is one-forth that of the small wheel

5 teeth

Four revolutions to one of the large wheel

**Gears** are toothed wheels and axles. Like all other machines, the gears can change the direction in which force is applied, or it can increase or decrease the force or distance over which force is applied. Gears need to work in pairs—a combination of two simple machines working together. When two or more simple machines work together to perform one task, it becomes a **compound machine**.

The screwdriver is a wheel and axle, since the handle is larger and represents the wheel that turns the shaft (axle) of the screwdriver. It is also important to note that the wheel is fixed to the axle and turns it directly. The **mechanical advantage** comes from the differential between the radius of the screwdriver handle and the radius of the screwdriver shaft. The force you apply in turning the handle of the screwdriver is traveling a much greater distance than the shaft and is, therefore, helping you do work.

If you can visualize the simple first-class lever and think of the rigid bar of the lever rotating around a point called the fulcrum, you have the basic idea for explaining how a wheel and axle works. If, in your first-class lever, you have the fulcrum closer to the resistance, the lever is helping you do

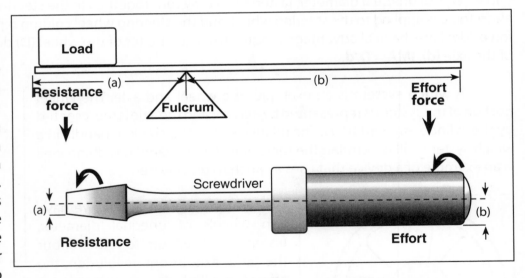

Load

Resistance force (a) (b) Effort force

Fulcrum

Screwdriver

(a) Resistance

(b) Effort

work and giving you a mechanical advantage. In our example, the radius of the central shaft of the screwdriver [(a) in the diagram] is analogous to the distance from the fulcrum to the resistance in the first-class lever. The radius of the screwdriver handle [(b) in the diagram] is analogous to the distance from the fulcrum to the effort in the first-class lever. The fulcrum in the screwdriver is represented by the central axis. Note: the effort and resistance are affected through rotation of the screwdriver.

Name: _____        Date: _____

# Quick Check

## Matching

_____ 1.  wheel and axle

_____ 2.  Fe

_____ 3.  compound machine

_____ 4.  gears

_____ 5.  Fr

a.  toothed wheels and axles

b.  force of the resistance

c.  force of the effort

d.  a wheel or crank rigidly attached to an axle

e.  two or more simple machines working together to perform one task

## Fill in the Blanks

6.  The force you apply in turning the handle of the screwdriver is traveling a much greater distance than the _____ and is, therefore, helping you do work.

7.  Gears need to work in pairs—a combination of two _____ machines working together.

8.  The _____ _____ comes from the differential between the radius of the screwdriver handle and the radius of the screwdriver shaft.

9.  A winch system is an example of a _____ and _____.

10.  The wheel and axle is another form of a _____.

## Multiple Choice

11.  Which of the following is NOT an example of a wheel and axle?

  a.  steering wheel

  b.  merry-go-round

  c.  escalator

  d.  screwdriver

12.  Which of the following is an example of a winch?

  a.  hand drill

  b.  steering wheel

  c.  wishing well

  d.  merry-go-round

13.  Which of the following is an example of a wheel and axle?

  a.  crowbar

  b.  wedge

  c.  screwdriver

  d.  chisel

Name: _____   Date: _____

# Knowledge Builder

## Activity: Wishing Well Winch

**Directions:**

1. Tape one end of a string at the center of the longer section of a flexible straw as shown at right. At the other end of the string, tie an open paper clip.

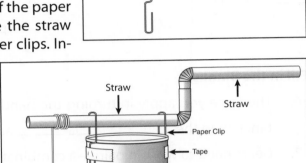

2. Open two other paper clips and tape them opposite each other on one end of a can with the larger loop of the paper clips extending up off the can as shown. Slide the straw with the string attached (axle) through the paper clips. Insert a second straw into the short end of the first straw and bend as shown. You have created a wheel and axle with the assembly of this crank or wheel.

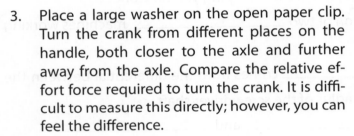

3. Place a large washer on the open paper clip. Turn the crank from different places on the handle, both closer to the axle and further away from the axle. Compare the relative effort force required to turn the crank. It is difficult to measure this directly; however, you can feel the difference.

4. In the illustration of your system below, label each of the components including the wheel, axle, resistance force (load), and effort force. Show the direction that the wheel is traveling and the resulting direction that the axle is turning.

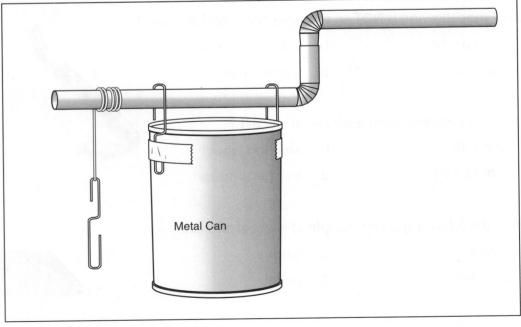

# Unit 6: Pulleys
## Teacher Information

**Topic:** A pulley is a kind of lever that can change the direction of a force and/or multiply force.

**Standards:**
>   **NSES** Unifying Concepts and Processes, (A), (B), (E), (F)
>   **NCTM** Geometry, Measurement, and Data Analysis and Probability
>   **STL** Technology and Society
>   See **National Standards** section (pages 62–66) for more information on each standard.

**Concepts:**
- Two factors must be considered when measuring work: (1) the force applied and (2) the distance through which the force acts.
- Mechanical advantages compare the force produced by a machine with the force applied to the machine.

**Naïve Concepts:**
- Force is a property of an object.
- A machine is a device that uses an energy source such as electricity, gas, or coal to do work.

**Science Process Skills:**

Students will be **making observations** about the operation of pulleys and **inferences** about the mechanical advantage and other uses for such a device. Students will **communicate** with others and **make predictions**; **describe** what will happen as they **manipulate materials to create models**; learn new words or unique uses of common words in relation to a given topic; **draw general conclusions** from particular details; and **record**, **interpret**, and **analyze data** gathered from **experiments** to **make decisions**.

**Lesson Planner:**
1. <u>Directed Reading</u>: Introduce the concepts and essential vocabulary relating to pulleys using the directed reading exercise on the Student Information page.
2. <u>Assessment</u>: Evaluate student comprehension of the information in the directed reading exercise using the quiz located on the Quick Check page.
3. <u>Concept Reinforcement</u>: Strengthen student understanding of concepts with the activities found on the Knowledge Builder pages. **Materials Needed**: Activity #1, #2, #3—2 thread spools, 6 paper clips, 1 meter of ribbon the same width as the spool, 2 bolts long enough to fit through the spools, 2 nuts to fit the bolts, cross bar (broom handle), 2 chairs to support cross bar, rubber band, 20 pennies, 2 small cups with a string attached to the top of each

**Extension:** Students research how pulleys have been used throughout history to help people make work easier.

**Real World Application:** Ancient people discovered they could harness the wind by adding sails to their ships. Pulleys were used to raise and lower the sails.

# Unit 6: Pulleys
## Student Information

A **pulley** is a kind of lever that can change the direction of force and/or multiply force. As shown in the diagrams, the effort force and effort movement are in the same direction. The resistance force is in the direction of gravity, and the resistance motion is in the opposite direction.

Pulleys can be set up in three different ways: a single fixed pulley, a movable pulley, or a block and tackle.

A **single fixed pulley** behaves like a first-class lever with the fulcrum (axis of the pulley) between the force and the load. The load moves up as the force goes down. This type of pulley only changes the direction of the force.

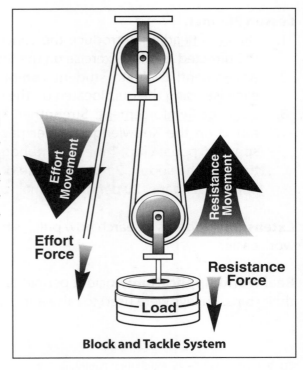

**Single Fixed Pulley**

A **movable pulley** is set up so the force and load move in the same direction. A moveable pulley resembles a second-class lever. The fulcrum is at the end of the lever where the supporting rope touches the pulley. The load is suspended from the pulley between the fulcrum and the force. The force in this type of pulley is multiplied.

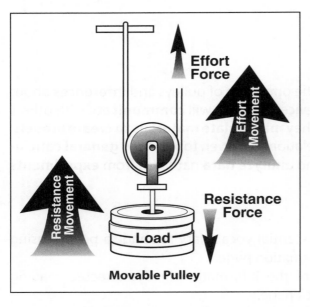

**Movable Pulley**

In a **block and tackle system**, pulleys can change the direction of a force and multiply the force. The block and tackle system consists of a fixed and a movable pulley. In a block and tackle system, the effort force moves downward as the load moves up. The number of lines determines how much the force is amplified.

**Block and Tackle System**

Name: _____    Date: _____

# Quick Check

## Matching

_____ 1.   single fixed pulley

a.   set up so the force and load move in the same direction

_____ 2.   pulley

_____ 3.   number of lines

b.   consists of a fixed and a movable pulley

c.   has the fulcrum (axis of the pulley) between the force and the load

_____ 4.   block and tackle

_____ 5.   movable pulley

d.   determines how much the force is amplified

e.   a kind of lever that can change the direction of force and/or multiply force

## Fill in the Blanks

6.   _____ can be set up in three different ways: a single fixed pulley, a movable pulley, or a block and tackle.

7.   In a pulley system, the effort _____ and effort _____ are in the same direction.

8.   In a block and tackle system, the effort force moves _____ as the load moves _____.

9.   With the pulley system, the resistance _____ is in the direction of gravity, and the resistance _____ is in the opposite direction.

10.  With a movable pulley, the _____ is at the end of the lever where the supporting rope touches the pulley.

## Multiple Choice

11.  What does a movable pulley resemble?

    a.   a second-class lever          b.   a first-class lever

    c.   a third-class lever            d.   a fourth-class lever

12.  What does a single fixed pulley behave like?

    a.   a fourth-class lever         b.   a third-class lever

    c.   a second-class lever        d.   a first-class lever

13.  This type of pulley only changes the direction of the force.

    a.   single fixed pulley         b.   block and tackle system

    c.   movable pulley             d.   second-class lever

Name: _____     Date: _____

# Knowledge Builder

## Activity #1: Fixed Pulley

**Directions:** Create a single fixed pulley as shown in the diagram.

<u>Part A</u>: Balance a crossbar (broom stick) between two chairs. Attach your pulley to the crossbar with a short length of string. Place a long ribbon over the spool. Measure the length of a rubber band before it is stretched. Record the length in the data table below. Attach two paper clips to the rubber band. Attach one of the paper clips to the string handle on a cup. Measure and record the length of the rubber band. Place 10 pennies in the cup. Lift the cup with pennies by picking it up

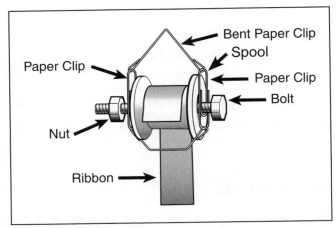

with the second paper clip. Measure and record the length of the rubber band. Using a paper clip, attach the string of the cup to one end of the ribbon that is over the pulley. Using a paper clip, attach the rubber band to the other end of the ribbon that is over the pulley. Pull on the rubber band to lift the cup. Measure and record the length of the rubber band in the data table.

<u>Part B</u>: Repeat the investigation three more times with different numbers of pennies.

| # of Pennies | Length Without Pulley | Length With Pulley | Difference |
|---|---|---|---|
| 0 | | | |
| 10 | | | |
| | | | |
| | | | |
| | | | |

Conclusions

1. Was there a difference between using the pulley and lifting the cup directly with the rubber band? _____

2. How does the fixed pulley affect the amount of effort needed to lift the cup with the pennies?

_____

_____

3. How does the fixed pulley affect the direction the force is applied to lift the cup with the pennies? _____

_____

Name: _____     Date: _____

# Knowledge Builder

## Activity #2: Movable Pulley

**Directions:** Create a movable pulley as shown in the diagram.

<u>Part A</u>: Balance a crossbar (broom stick) between two chairs. Attach one end of the ribbon to the crossbar (broom handle). Place the ribbon under the spool. Measure and record the length of the rubber band in the data table. Attach two paper clips to the rubber band. Attach one of the paper clips attached to the rubber band to the string on the cup. Using the other paper clip on the rubber band, pick up the cup. Measure and record the length of the rubber band in the data table. Place 5 pennies in the cup. Lift the cup with pennies with the rubber band, and record the length of the

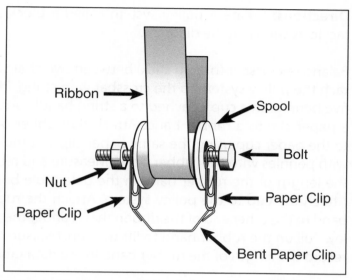

rubber band. Attach the cup to the pulley. Attach the rubber band to the free end of the ribbon that is under the pulley. Pull on the rubber band to lift the cup. Measure and record the length of the rubber band in the data table.

<u>Part B</u>: Repeat the investigation three more times with different numbers of pennies.

| # of Pennies | Length Without Pulley | Length With Pulley | Difference |
|:---:|:---:|:---:|:---:|
| 0 | | | |
| 5 | | | |
| | | | |
| | | | |
| | | | |

Conclusions

1.  Was there a difference between using the pulley and lifting the cup directly with the rubber band? _____

2.  How does the movable pulley affect the amount of effort needed to lift the cup with the pennies? _____ _____

3.  How does the movable pulley affect the direction the force is applied to lift the cup with the pennies? _____ _____

Name: _____    Date: _____

# Knowledge Builder

## Activity #3: Create a Pulley System

**Directions:** Create a pulley system called a block and tackle as shown in the diagram.

Balance a crossbar (broom stick) between two chairs. Attach the pulley system to the crossbar with string. Place five pennies in a cup attached to a string handle. Attach a paper clip to a rubber band. Attach the rubber band to the paper cup using the same paper clip. Lift the cup with pennies with the rubber band. Measure and record the length of the rubber band in the data table below. Attach the cup to the pulley system. Attach the rubber band to the other end of the ribbon that is under the pulley. Pull on the rubber band to lift the cup. Measure and record the length of the rubber band in the data table.

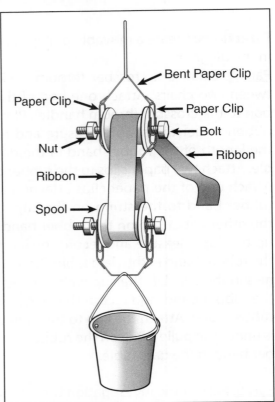

| # of Lines | Length Without Pulley | Length With Pulley | Difference |
|---|---|---|---|
| 0 | | | |
| 2 | | | |

Conclusions

1. Was there a difference between using the pulley system and lifting the cup directly with the rubber band? _____

2. How does the block and tackle affect the amount of effort needed to lift the cup with the pennies? _____

3. How does the block and tackle affect the direction the force is applied to lift the cup with the pennies? _____

# Unit 7: Gears
## Teacher Information

**Topic:** A gear system includes levers and the wheel and axle.

**Standards:**
**NSES** Unifying Concepts and Processes, (A), (B), (E), (F), (G)
**NCTM** Geometry, Measurement, and Data Analysis and Probability
**STL** Technology and Society
See **National Standards** section (pages 62–66) for more information on each standard.

**Concepts:**
- A compound machine is made of two or more simple machines working together to accomplish a task.
- A compound machine helps us do work.

**Naïve Concepts:**
- A machine is a device that uses an energy source such as electricity, gas, or coal to do work.

**Science Process Skills:**

Students will **make observations** about the operation of gears. Students will **make inferences** about the mechanical advantage and use of gears. Students will **make inferences** about the relationship of the gear to the wheel and axle and the lever. Students will **apply knowledge** to the identification of examples of gears in compound machines. Students will **measure** the relative effort needed to move or turn a resistance or load, **collect and record data**, **identify and control variables**, **predict**, **interpret data**, and **apply the information** to examples outside the classroom.

**Lesson Planner:**
1. <u>Directed Reading</u>: Introduce the concepts and essential vocabulary relating to gears using the directed reading exercise found on the Student Information page.
2. <u>Assessment</u>: Evaluate student comprehension of the information in the directed reading exercise using the quiz located on the Quick Check page.
3. <u>Concept Reinforcement</u>: Strengthen student understanding of concepts with the activities found on the Knowledge Builder pages. **Materials Needed:** Activity #1—8 cm diameter cardboard mailing tube, a 3.5 cm diameter wrapping paper tube, corrugated cardboard, smooth on one side and ribbed on the other (check art supply store), foam board, T-pins or small nails, glue, heavy tag board, scissors; Activity #2—2 10-speed bikes, watch with second hand, pair of roller skates

**Extension:** Students research the evolution of gears and their importance to humankind.

**Real World Application:** Early gears were made from wood and lubricated with animal fat. Today, our electronics are made with lubricant-free plastic gears.

# Unit 7: Gears
## Student Information

**Gears** are toothed wheels and axles. The gear is a compound machine with elements of the lever in both the tooth-to-tooth interaction between the gear teeth and the transmission of power from one wheel to another, as in a wheel and axle. Like all other machines, the gears can change the direction in which the force is applied, or it can increase or decrease the force or distance over which the force is applied. Gears need to work in pairs—a combination of two simple machines working together. When two or more simple machines work together to perform one task, it becomes a **compound machine**.

Many devices have gears. Examples include analog clocks, hand mixers, automobile transmissions, bicycles, music boxes, and many electric motors.

**Gear wheels** may be the same size or may vary in size. The movement of gears may be modeled by imagining two wheels with their faces in contact with each other, one driving the other. The wheels have grooves or teeth cut into the surface to eliminate slippage. Gear wheel combinations of different diameters, as in the diagram below, are used to increase or decrease speed. If we apply the effort force to the larger wheel we gain speed, since the second wheel will make four revolutions while the first is making one.

Two or more gears meshed together are called a **gear train**. The gear on which the force is applied is the **driver**, and the other gear is the **driven gear**. Any gears between the driver and the driven gear are called **idlers**. The gear wheels are meshed together to make one turn the other, so they will turn in opposite directions. The number of teeth on the gear will determine the number of rotations it takes to turn the other gear. If a large gear has 20 teeth and it is meshed with a smaller gear with 5 teeth, the smaller gear turns four times for every one turn of the larger gear. The larger gear multiples the force. Doing the same amount of work, it takes one-fourth less force to move the same distance.

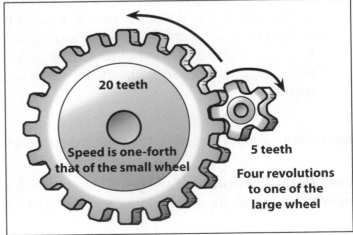

20 teeth

Speed is one-forth that of the small wheel

5 teeth

**Four revolutions to one of the large wheel**

Gears are used to transfer power from one shaft to another to change the direction of rotation and speed. Specialized gears may be used to reorient shaft rotation to nonparallel and non-intersecting axes. See the diagram below of the straight-miter bevel gear and the worm gear compared to the simple parallel spur gear train.

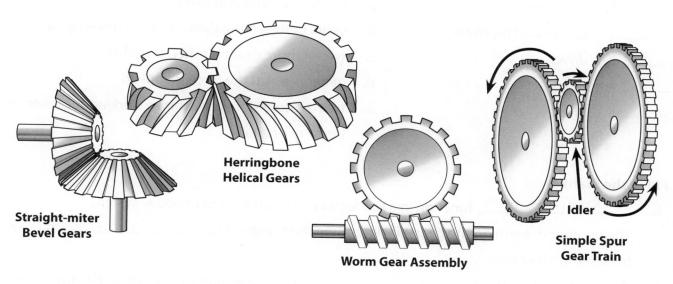

**Straight-miter Bevel Gears**

**Herringbone Helical Gears**

**Worm Gear Assembly**

**Idler**

**Simple Spur Gear Train**

Gears function in a similar way to a belt system or pulley system. In a belt system, force is transferred through a belt from one wheel to another. There is some tension on the belt as it passes over each wheel, and the system relies on friction between the belt and each wheel. A pulley system may consist of one fixed wheel or one movable wheel with a rope over the pulley wheel. An operator pulls on one end of the line (effort force), with the other end on the line attached to an object that is to be moved or lifted (resistance force or load). Gears differ in that each gear wheel has teeth that are in direct contact with another gear wheel or wheels. The teeth are used to avoid slippage and to transfer force directly. Gears are a combination of the wheel and axle and levers (teeth). Gears lined together in chains have the same pattern of turning as belts or pulleys.

There are two basic phenomena to observe in a gear chain: the **direction of rotation** in each gear wheel and the **change in speed** of each gear. First, as one gear turns, it makes contact with a second gear that turns in the opposite direction. A third gear in the system will turn in the same direction as the first gear. Second, speed may be determined by measuring the diameter of each gear wheel or by counting teeth.

Example:

- The first gear has 40 teeth, and the second gear has 10 teeth, the ratio is 40/10 or 4/1.

- The **turn ratio** is said to be 1 to 4, and the **mechanical advantage** is the same as the **teeth ratio** or 4. Note that the teeth ratio and the mechanical advantage (ratio or output to input) are the inverse of the turn ratio.

**Simple Machines**

Name: _____ Date: _____

# Quick Check

## Matching

_____ 1.  gear train

_____ 2.  compound machine

_____ 3.  driver

_____ 4.  gears

_____ 5.  idlers

a.  toothed wheels and axles

b.  gears between the driver and the driven gear

c.  two or more gears meshed together

d.  gear on which the force is applied

e.  two or more simple machines working together to perform one task

## Fill in the Blanks

6.  _____ function in a similar way to a belt system or pulley system.

7.  The number of teeth on the gear will determine the number of _____ it takes to turn the other gear.

8.  Gears are used to transfer _____ from one shaft to another to change the direction of _____ and _____.

9.  Gear wheel combinations of different diameters are used to _____ or _____ speed.

10.  The gear is a _____ _____ with elements of the lever in both the tooth-to-tooth interaction between the gear teeth and the transmission of power from one wheel to another as in a wheel and axle.

## Multiple Choice

11.  Which of the following is NOT an example of a machine that uses gears?

a.  clock

b.  swing

c.  bicycle

d.  music box

12.  What is the gear a combination of?

a.  lever and wedge

b.  wedge and pulley

c.  wheel and axle and levers

d.  screw and pulley

13.  If the first gear has 40 teeth, and the second gear has 10 teeth, what is the teeth ratio?

a.  40/1

b.  6/1

c.  4/10

d.  4/1

Name: _____ Date: _____

# Knowledge Builder

## Activity #1: Gear System

**Directions:** First cut a large cardboard mailing tube (8-cm diameter) and a small wrapping paper tube (3.5-cm diameter) into 2-cm wheels. Cut a sheet of corrugated cardboard into 2-cm wide strips. The strips need to be cut across the corrugation ribs. Think of each rib as a tooth in your gear. The edge of your strip should look like the one in the diagram.

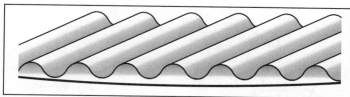

Next, glue the corrugated strips with the smooth side glued to the outside surfaces of the large wheel and the small wheel. The ribbing should be facing out like a tire tread on both wheels. Fill the centers of the wheels with foam board disks. They should fit snugly. Find the center of each gear wheel, and put a T-pin through the center. The T-pin becomes your axle.

Now label one gear "A" and the other gear "B." Turn the gear wheels against each other and observe the direction of the turn and the number of turns each makes.

Complete the data table below for each gear.

| Gear | Number of Teeth | Wheel Diameter | Direction of Rotation |
|---|---|---|---|
| Gear A | | | |
| Gear B | | | |

Conclusions

1. What is the teeth ratio? (Hint: If the first gear has 40 teeth and the second gear has 10 teeth, the ratio is 40/10 or 4/1.) _____

2. What direction does Gear A turn relative to Gear B? _____

3. How many turns are observed in Gear B when Gear A is rotated one time? _____

4. How many turns are observed in Gear A when Gear B is rotated one time? _____

5. What is the turn ratio of Gear A to Gear B? (Hint: If the teeth ratio is 4/1, then the turn ratio is said to be 1 to 4.) _____

Name: _____     Date: _____

# Knowledge Builder

## Activity #2: Analyzing Bicycle Gears

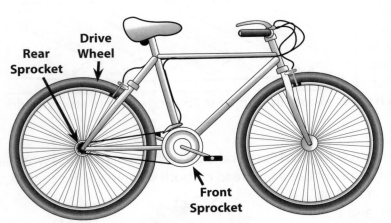

If you have a "ten-speed" bicycle, you've probably realized by now that it doesn't have ten "speeds" at all. After all, you can change the speed of your bike by just pedaling faster or slower—no matter which "speed" it's set for. What it really has is ten different gear combinations that make it easier for you to start up, pedal up a hill, or go fast on level ground.

You know that pushing the pedals of your bike turns the large gear wheel, or front sprocket. The moving teeth of the front sprocket pull the endless drive chain, which turns a small rear sprocket (located on the back wheel hub). The rear sprocket then turns the hub of the rear wheel, or drive wheel, pushing the bike along.

**Directions:** Here are four different tests to find out how the different gear ratios on your bike affect your bicycling.

Test #1:  Mark off a distance of 6 meters on the pavement. Have a partner time you as you go from a dead stop to a distance of 6 meters, first in the lowest gear and then in a higher gear. Which was faster? _____

Test #2:  Have a partner time you from a stop to the length of a whole block, first in first or low gear, then in high, then using all ten gears in order. Which way was the fastest? _____ Explain why? _____

_____

Test #3:  Start your bicycles from rest, with your own in high gear and your partner's in low gear. Who seems to be working harder? _____ Who will seem to work harder if you come to a hill? _____

Test #4:  The "pulling power" that gear ratio gives you is called traction. Have your partner hold onto the rear of your bicycle while wearing roller skates. Does higher gear give you enough traction to start your bike? _____ Can you do it in a middle gear? _____ Which gear makes it easier? _____

Adapted from: Lefkowitz, R.J. (October 16, 1967). "Big gears, little gears." *Nature and Science Journal.*

# Unit 8: Belt Systems
## Teacher Information

**Topic:** A belt system includes a wheel and axle and pulley.

**Standards:**
**NSES** Unifying Concepts and Processes, (A), (B), (E), (F), (G)
**NCTM** Geometry and Data Analysis and Probability
**STL** Technology and Society
See **National Standards** section (pages 62–66) for more information on each standard.

**Concepts:**
- A compound machine is made of two or more simple machines working together to accomplish a task.
- A compound machine helps us do work.

**Naïve Concepts:**
- A machine is a device that uses an energy source such as electricity, gas, or coal to do work.

**Science Process Skills:**

Students will **make observations** about the direction of rotation and speed of rotation of spools, **inferences** about the mechanical advantage, effects of friction, force, speed, and distance through which a force acts; **classify** various examples of belt systems; **apply knowledge** to the identification of examples of the use of belts in compound machines; **measure** the relative effort needed to move a resistance or load; **collect and record data**; **identify and control variables**; **predict**; and **interpret data**.

**Lesson Planner:**
1. <u>Directed Reading</u>: Introduce the concepts and essential vocabulary relating to belt systems using the directed reading exercise on the Student Information pages.
2. <u>Assessment</u>: Evaluate student comprehension of the information in the directed reading exercise using the quiz located on the Quick Check page.
3. <u>Concept Reinforcement</u>: Strengthen student understanding of concepts with the activities found on the Knowledge Builder pages. **Materials Needed:** thread spools (of varying sizes), rubber bands, pegboard the size of a sheet of paper (8" x 11"), nails (size of spool openings)

**Extension:** Students research the belt system and compile a list of its uses.

**Real World Application:** A belt system is often used to convey coal from the mine face to the mouth of the mine. You have probably seen belt systems working at the checkout lane in a grocery store.

# Unit 8: Belt Systems
## Student Information

A **belt system** is a compound machine made up of the wheel and axle and pulley. The combination of the wheel and axle and the pulley depends on how the belt system is configured. They are also related to gears. Think of the wheels in a pulley system as gears without teeth. There are sev- eral types of wheels. If the wheel spins freely and is fairly smooth, it is a simple wheel. If the wheel is attached to the axle and either drives the axle or is driven by the axle, it is a wheel and axle. If your car is a front-wheel-drive vehicle, then the front wheels represent a wheel and axle system, and the rear wheels are simple wheels. If the wheel has teeth, then it is a gear. If the wheel has a groove down the center, then it is a pulley.

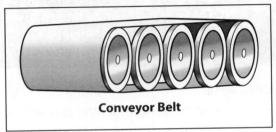

**Conveyor Belt**

A **simple belt system** consists of two pulley wheels and a belt. When one pulley wheel is turned, the energy is transferred through the belt to the second wheel. The belt system relies on friction between the belt and the pulley wheels. Note that a belt set up in a crossed pattern will be in contact with a greater portion of the wheels; therefore, it is less likely to slip. Sometimes, we think that friction is working against us in a machine system. This is an example of the need for some friction for the system to function properly.

The **relative size** of the pulleys in a belt system will determine the mechanical advantage. The arrangement of the belts determines the direction the wheels will rotate. A belt looped around two pulleys in a **parallel arrangement** will cause both wheels to rotate in the same direction. A belt looped around two pulleys in a **crossed pattern arrangement** will cause the wheels to rotate in opposite directions.

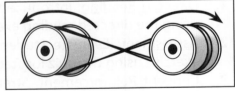

Examples of belts include the fan belt in a car, the belt system on a table saw, the belt on a sewing machine, the belt system in a lawn tractor, and the conveyor belt in a factory.

Simple Machines                                                    Unit 8: Belt Systems

Name: _____   Date: _____

# Quick Check

## Matching

_____ 1.   cross pattern arrangement

_____ 2.   belt system

_____ 3.   relative size of pulleys

_____ 4.   parallel arrangement

_____ 5.   simple belt system

a.   causes the wheels to rotate in opposite directions

b.   consists of two pulley wheels and a belt

c.   causes both wheels to rotate in the same direction

d.   a compound machine made up of the wheel and axle and pulley

e.   determines the mechanical advantage

## Fill in the Blanks

6.   The belt looped around two pulleys in a _____ arrangement will cause both wheels to rotate in the same direction.

7.   A belt looped around two pulleys in a _____ pattern or arrangement will cause the wheels to rotate in opposite directions.

8.   The belt system relies on _____ between the belt and the pulley wheels.

9.   If your car is a front-wheel-drive vehicle, then the front wheels represent a_____ and _____ system, and the rear wheels are _____ wheels.

10.  A simple belt system consists of two pulley wheels and a belt. When one pulley wheel is turned, the _____ is transferred through the belt to the _____ wheel.

## Multiple Choice

11.  Which of the following does NOT have a belt system?
     a.   lawn tractor              b.   fishing rod
     c.   sewing machine            d.   table saw

12.  What is a wheel with teeth called?
     a.   pulley                    b.   gear
     c.   screw                     d.   lever

13.  What is a wheel with a groove down the center called?
     a.   gear                      b.   pulley
     c.   lever                     d.   screw

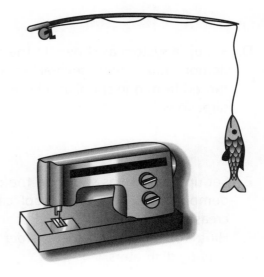

Name: _____     Date: _____

# Knowledge Builder

## Activity: Constructing Belt Systems

**Directions:** Using spools (wheels), nails, pegboard, and rubber bands (belts), set up a belt system as shown in each diagram below. In the data table on page 45, make a sketch of each system that you developed and describe what is observed in terms of the direction that each wheel in the system turns and any difference in speed observed in each wheel of the system. Include labels (numbers or letters of the alphabet) for each of the wheels (spools) in the system. Show the belt and use arrows to indicate the direction that the belt is traveling and the resulting direction that each wheel is turning.

A. Set up a two-spool system as shown in the diagram that demonstrates that a belt system can be used to turn a second spool in the same direction as the first spool.

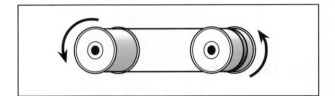

B. Set up a two-spool system as shown in the diagram that demonstrates that a belt system can be used to turn a second spool in the opposite direction as the first spool.

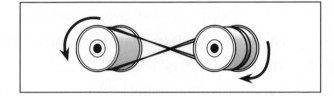

C. Set up a system as shown in the diagram that demonstrates that several spools may be turned from one spool.

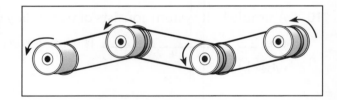

D. Set up a system as shown in the diagram that demonstrates that several spools may be turned from one spool and in several different directions.

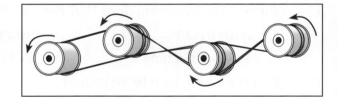

E. Set up a system as shown in the diagram that demonstrates how one spool can either increase or decrease the speed of another spool. Hint: You may need to consider spools with varying diameters.

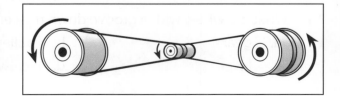

Name: _____ Date: _____

# Knowledge Builder

## Activity: Constructing Belt Systems (cont.)

**Exploration/Data Collection Chart:** The first system is done for you as an example.

| Brief description of each system | Sketch of your system | Predict the direction of rotation of each wheel and the speed of rotation. | Observed direction of rotation of each wheel and the speed of rotation of each wheel. |
|---|---|---|---|
| Example: Two wheels of equal diameter with parallel belt setup. | | The wheels will turn in the same direction and speed. | The wheels turn in the same direction and at the same speed. |
| | | | |
| | | | |
| | | | |
| | | | |

# Unit 9: Inclined Planes
## Teacher Information

**Topic:** The inclined plane is a device that allows us to increase the height of an object without lifting it vertically.

**Standards:**
   **NSES** Unifying Concepts and Processes, (A), (B), (E), (F), (G)
   **NCTM** Number and Operations, Algebra, and Measurement
   **STL** Technology and Society
   See **National Standards** section (pages 62–66) for more information on each standard.

**Concepts:**
- Two factors must be considered when measuring work: (1) the force applied and (2) the distance through which the force acts.
- Mechanical advantage compares the force produced by a machine with the force applied to the machine.

**Naïve Concepts:**
- Force is a property of an object.
- A machine is a device that uses an energy source such as electricity, gas, or coal to do work.

**Science Process Skills:**
   Students will **make observations** about the relative force needed to move an object up slopes of varying degrees and **make inferences** about the mechanical advantage and the direction, force, and distance through which a force acts; **classify** various examples of tools into one or several of the simple machines that they represent; and **measure** the relative effort needed to move a resistance (load).

**Lesson Planner:**
1. Directed Reading: Introduce the concepts and essential vocabulary relating to inclined planes using the directed reading exercise found on the Student Information page.
2. Assessment: Evaluate student comprehension of the information in the directed reading exercise using the quiz located on the Quick Check page.
3. Concept Reinforcement: Strengthen student understanding of concepts with the activities found on the Knowledge Builder page. **Materials Needed:** Activity #1—meter stick, metal washers, 30-cm rulers, small margarine tub, several large paper clips, 50-cm string, several books, triple-beam balance, Newton pull-type spring scale; Activity #2—books, wooden plank 1–2 meters in length, Newton pull-type spring scale, meter stick, toy car
4. Inquiry Investigation: Determine if mass affects the speed of a toy car rolling down a ramp. Divide the class into teams. Instruct each team to complete the Inquiry Investigation pages.

**Extension:** Students research the history of inclined planes. They identify the earliest inclined planes, people who used them, and how they were being used.

**Real World Application:** Inclined planes, such as ramps, make life easier for many people. Ramps permit people using wheeled objects, such as wheelchairs, strollers, and carts, to more easily access buildings.

# Unit 9: Inclined Planes
## Student Information

One group of simple machines is the inclined plane family. An **inclined plane** is a flat, sloping surface over which objects may be rolled or slid to a higher level. It is a simple machine that reduces the force required to move an object over a vertical distance or height. It allows a person to exert less force to move an object; however, the total amount of

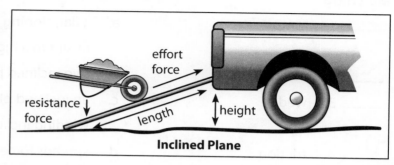

**Inclined Plane**

work is not reduced, since the force is spread over a longer distance. Think of it this way: it's easier to climb a set of stairs to get to a second floor than it is to scale a wall or climb a rope straight up. The **Ideal Mechanical Advantage (IMA)** for the inclined plane is equal to the length of the slope divided by the height of the plane or **IMA= l/h**.

**Friction** is a force that resists motion. It can reduce the amount of work that can be done with a given force. Friction is an important consideration in sliding or rolling an object up a ramp or inclined plane. The longer and more gradual the slope of the inclined plane, the less force is needed to move an object up the slope. Note that as the slope decreases, the friction increases between the object being moved up the slope and the surface of the inclined plane. There are two ways to vary the slope of an inclined plane: you can either increase or decrease the length or the height of the inclined plane. Ideally, the work required to lift an object directly is the same as the work required to move an object up an inclined plane.

Inclined planes can be divided into three different types: the ramp, the wedge, and the screw or bolt.

A **ramp** spreads the force over a longer distance, so it takes less force to lift an object. As shown in the diagram above, the effort force and effort movement are in the same direction. The resistance force is in the direction of gravity, and the resistance motion is in the opposite direction. Examples are stairs, escalators, handicap ramps, and skateboard ramps.

**Ramp**

A **wedge** is two inclined planes put back-to-back. Like the ramp, the wedge spreads the force needed to move the load over a longer distance. Examples are a knife, an ax, the point of a needle, a nail, and scissor blades.

**Wedge**

A **bolt or screw** is an inclined plane wrapped around a central point or a winding inclined plane. Examples of winding inclined planes are a spiral staircase, drill bit threads, wood screw threads, bolts, and pigtail curves in the mountains. The wood screw and drill bit are compound machines because the threads are inclined planes, but there is a wedge on the points.

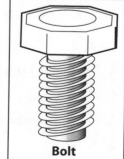

**Bolt**

Name: _____     Date: _____

# Quick Check

## Matching

_____ 1.   ramp

_____ 2.   inclined plane

_____ 3.   wedge

_____ 4.   friction

_____ 5.   screw or bolt

a.   a flat, sloping surface over which objects may be rolled or slid to a higher level

b.   two inclined planes put back-to-back

c.   an inclined plane wrapped around a central point or a winding inclined plane

d.   spreads force over a longer distance

e.   force that resists motion

## Fill in the Blanks

6.   An inclined plane is a _____ _____ that reduces the force required to move an object over a vertical distance or height.

7.   Friction is an important consideration in sliding or rolling an object up a _____ or inclined plane.

8.   The resistance force is in the direction of _____, and the resistance motion is in the opposite direction.

9.   Like the ramp, the _____ spreads the force needed to move the load over a longer distance.

10.   The wood screw and drill bit are _____ _____ because the threads are inclined planes, but there is a wedge on the points.

## Multiple Choice

11.   Which of the following is NOT an example of a bolt or screw?

    a.   pigtail curve in the mountains

    b.   drill bit threads

    c.   escalator

    d.   wood screw

12.   Which of the following is NOT an example of a wedge?

    a.   point of a needle

    b.   knife

    c.   ax

    d.   stairs

13.   Which of the following is NOT an example of a ramp?

    a.   nail

    b.   stairs

    c.   handicap ramp

    d.   escalator

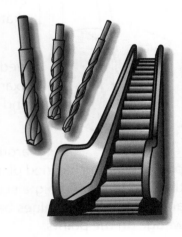

Name: _____    Date: _____

# Knowledge Builder

## Activity #1: Force, Mass, and the Inclined Plane

**Directions:** Make three stacks of books of varying heights. Place the stacks on the floor. Use 30-cm metric rulers as your inclined plane and the 3 different stacks of books to support the ruler of each inclined plane. Record the height of each stack of books in centimeters in the data table below. Attach one end of a 50-cm piece of yarn to a small margarine tub that has a mass of 500 grams. (Place the tub on a triple-beam balance and add washers until the mass is 500.) Attach the other end of the string to a Newton pull-type spring scale. Use the spring scale to pull the tub up each of the three inclined planes. Measure the amount of force needed to move the mass up each inclined plane to the top. Record the force in the data table below.

| Inclined Planes | | |
| --- | --- | --- |
| | **Height** | **Force in Newtons (N)** |
| Inclined Plane #1 | | |
| Inclined Plane #2 | | |
| Inclined Plane #3 | | |

Conclusion

Why is there a difference in the effort needed to move a mass up the inclined planes?

_____

_____

## Activity #2: W = F x d

**Directions:** Construct a ramp using a stack of books and a wooden plank. Measure and record the length of the ramp in the data table. Attach the Newton pull-type spring scale to the toy car and place the car at the end of the ramp as shown in the diagram. Pull the car up the ramp to the top of the stack. Record the force needed to pull the car up the ramp in the data table. Use the formula W = F x d to calculate how much work was done. Repeat the activity two more times. Use different length planks each time.

| | **Distance (m)** | **Force (N)** | **Work (W = F x d)** |
| --- | --- | --- | --- |
| Plank #1 | | | |
| Plank #2 | | | |
| Plank #3 | | | |

Conclusion

How does the distance an object moves over a ramp affect the amount of work done?

_____

_____

Name: _____   Date: _____

# Inquiry Investigation: Mass and Speed

**Concept:**
- Two factors must be considered when measuring work: (1) the force applied and (2) the distance through which the force acts.

**Purpose:** Does mass affect the speed of a toy car rolling down a ramp?

**Hypothesis:** Write a sentence that predicts what you think will happen in the experiment. Your hypothesis should be clearly written. It should answer the question stated in the purpose.

Hypothesis: _____

_____

**Procedure:** Carry out the investigation. This includes gathering the materials, following the step-by-step directions, and recording the data.

**Materials:**

| | | |
|---|---|---|
| toy car | stopwatch | calculator |
| meter stick | 3 books | 3 pennies |
| tape | ramp (at least 1 meter long) | |
| triple beam-balance | | |

**Experiment:**

Step 1:   Find the mass of the car and record it in the data table under Car #1. Stack the three books on the floor. Place one end of the ramp on the books and the other on the floor. Place the rear wheels of the car at the top end of the ramp. Release the car as you start the stopwatch. Stop timing when the front of the car gets to the bottom of the ramp. Record the time in the data table under Car #1. Repeat the procedure two more times. Calculate the speed of your car by using the formula above. Then find the average of the three speeds for Car #1.

$$speed = \frac{distance}{time}$$

Step 2:   Tape the pennies on top of the car. Find the mass and record in the data table under Car #2. Place the rear wheels of the car at the top end of the ramp. Release the car as you start the stopwatch. Stop timing when the front of the car gets to the bottom of the ramp. Record the time in the data table under Car #2. Repeat the procedure two more times. Calculate the speed and record in the data table. Then find the average of the three speeds for Car #2.

**Results:** Record the mass, time, and distance in the data table on the next page. Calculate the speed and the average speed and record in the data table for each car.

Name: _____     Date: _____

| Trial # | Car #1 | | | | Car #2 (with pennies) | | | |
|---|---|---|---|---|---|---|---|---|
| | Mass (g) | Distance (cm) | Time (s) | Speed (cm/s) | Mass (g) | Distance (cm) | Time (s) | Speed (cm/s) |
| #1 | | | | | | | | |
| #2 | | | | | | | | |
| #3 | | | | | | | | |
| | Average speed: _____ | | | | Average speed: _____ | | | |

**Analysis:** Study the results of your experiment. Decide what the data means. This information can then be used to help you draw a conclusion about what you learned in your investigation.

Use your data to create a graph that will compare the mass and the average speed of the toy cars. Place the average speed of the cars on the *y*-axis. Place the mass of the cars on the *x*-axis.

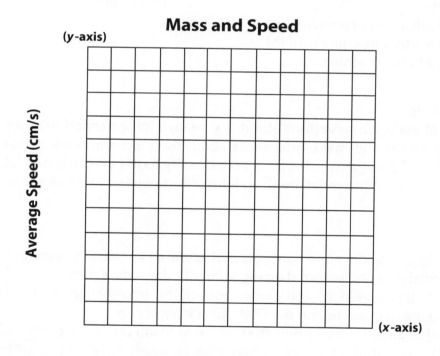

**Mass and Speed**

(*y*-axis)

Average Speed (cm/s)

(*x*-axis)

Car Mass (g)

**Conclusion:**
Write a description of what actually happened in the experiment and whether or not the hypothesis was supported by the data collected.

_____

_____

_____

_____

# Unit 10: Wedges
## Teacher Information

**Topic:** The wedge is a modification of the inclined plane.

**Standards:**
    **NSES** Unifying Concepts and Processes, (A), (B), (E), (F), (G)
    **NCTM** Numbers and Operations, Algebra, Geometry, and Measurement
    **STL** Technology and Society
    See **National Standards** section (pages 62–66) for more information on each standard.

**Concepts:**
- Two factors must be considered when measuring work: (1) the force applied, and (2) the distance through which the force acts.
- Mechanical advantage compares the force produced by a machine with the force applied to the machine.

**Naïve Concepts:**
- Force is a property of an object.
- A machine is a device that uses an energy source such as electricity, gas, or coal to do work.

**Science Process Skills:**

Students will **make observations** about the relative force needed to move an object with wedges of varying widths and **make inferences** about the mechanical advantage and the direction, force, and distance through which a force acts; **classify** tools into categories related to inclined planes, wedges, and screws; and **measure** the relative effort needed to move a resistance (load).

**Lesson Planner:**
1. Directed Reading: Introduce the concepts and essential vocabulary relating to wedges using the directed reading exercise found on the Student Information page.
2. Assessment: Evaluate student comprehension of the information in the directed reading exercise using the quiz located on the Quick Check page.
3. Concept Reinforcement: Strengthen student understanding of concepts with the activities found on the Knowledge Builder pages. **Materials Needed:** Activity #1—cardboard, protractor, Newton pull-type spring scales, scissors, paper clip, 30-cm ruler, books; Activity #2—two large nails (one with and one without a point), hammer, board, 30-cm ruler

**Extension:** Until the 1800s, nails were handmade one by one. Students research nails to discover how the manufacturing of nails has changed throughout history.

**Real World Application:** In Europe during the Middle Ages, men carried their own knives to eat with, and they were expected to cut food for the women present during meals.

# Unit 10: Wedges
## Student Information

A **wedge** is the name of any object with at least one slanting side, ending in a sharp edge, which cuts material apart. The wedge is a modification of the inclined plane. Like the ramp, the wedge spreads the force needed to move the load over a longer distance. The wedge is actually a kind of mobile inclined plane. The sharper the edge of the wedge, the less effort force is needed to overcome resistance. A **double wedge** (shown at the left) is two inclined planes put back-to-back.

The zipper used on clothing has a slider that includes an upper triangular wedge for opening the zipper and two lower wedges that close the teeth of the zipper. Examples of wedges include knives, axes, needles, nails, and chisels.

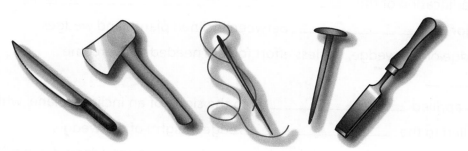

There are two major differences between inclined planes and wedges. (1) An inclined plane remains stationary, while the wedge moves. (2) The effort force is applied parallel to the slope of an inclined plane, while the effort force is applied to the vertical edge (height) of the wedge.

The **ideal mechanical advantage (IMA)** of a wedge is determined by dividing the length of the incline by the width of the wedge at its thickest point. The wedge with the longest incline relative to its width at the thickest part will require the least force to separate or split something. The Ideal Mechanical Advantage (IMA) for the inclined plane is equal to the length of the slope divided by the height of the plane or **IMA = l/h**.

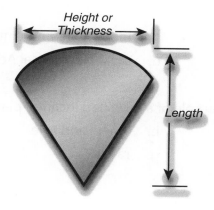

Height or Thickness

Length

Name: _____ Date: _____

# Quick Check

**Matching**

_____ 1. inclined plane

_____ 2. wedge

_____ 3. nail

_____ 4. ideal mechanical advantage

_____ 5. double wedge

a. the name of any object with at least one slanting side, ending in a sharp edge, which cuts material apart

b. example of a wedge

c. remains stationary

d. two inclined planes put back-to-back

e. determined by dividing the length of the incline by the width of the wedge at its thickest point

**Fill in the Blanks**

6. The wedge is a modification of the _____ _____.

7. There are two major _____ between inclined planes and wedges.

8. The sharper the edge of the wedge, the less effort force is needed to overcome _____.

9. The effort force is applied _____ to the slope of an inclined plane, while the effort force is applied to the _____ edge (height) of the wedge.

10. The zipper used on clothing has a slider that includes an upper triangular wedge for _____ the zipper and two lower _____ that close the teeth of the zipper.

**Multiple Choice**

11. Which of the following is NOT an example of a wedge?

   a. nail

   b. knife

   c. escalator

   d. ax

12. What does IMA stand for?

   a. Ideas Make Advantage

   b. Ideal Money Advantage

   c. Ideal Machine Advantage

   d. Ideal Mechanical Advantage

13. Which of the following is an example of a modified inclined plane?

   a. lever

   b. wheel and axle

   c. wedge

   d. ramp

Name: _____  Date: _____

# Knowledge Builder

## Activity #1: Making and Using Wedges

**Directions:** Make three double wedges out of corrugated cardboard: one with an overall angular width of 20 degrees, a second with a width of 40 degrees, and a third with a width of 60 degrees. Cut out and trace around the patterns below to make the three wedges.

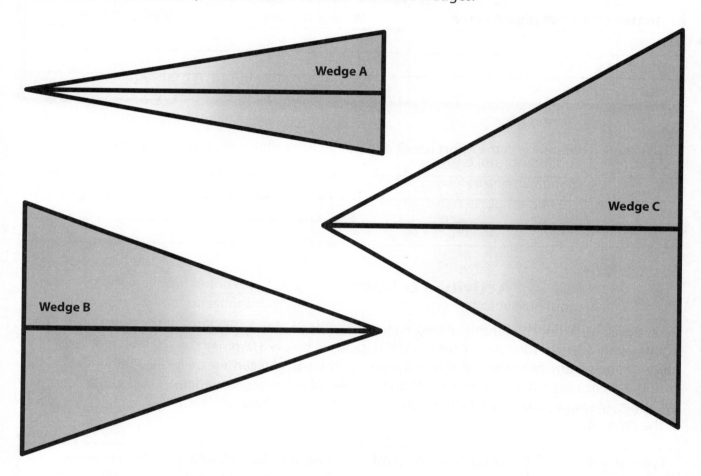

Now, attach a large paper clip to the tip of each of the wedges. Using a Newton pull-type spring scale, pull each wedge between two large books and determine the relative force needed to separate the books with each wedge model. As you pull each wedge between the books, note the amount of force needed to separate the two books on the spring scale. (If your spring scale is in grams or ounces, you are estimating force, since force is measured in newtons.) Record the measurement in the data table on the next page.

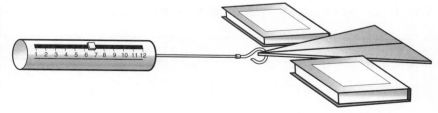

Name: _____    Date: _____

# Knowledge Builder

## Activity #1: Making and Using Wedges (cont.)

Results: The data should be collected in three trials for each wedge. Record your data in the table below.

| Trials | Wedge A Force | Wedge B Force | Wedge C Force |
|---|---|---|---|
| Trial #1 | | | |
| Trial #2 | | | |
| Trial #3 | | | |

Conclusion

Why is there a difference in the effort needed to move the wedge between the books?

_____

_____

_____

_____

## Activity #2: Nails

**Directions:** Measure the length of two nails (one with and one without a point) using a 30-cm ruler and record in the data table below. Hammer the nail with the wedge five times. Measure the part of the nail you can see. Record the measurement in centimeters. Hammer the nail without the wedge five times. Measure the part of the nail you can see. Record the measurement in the data table.

| Type of Nail | Length of Nail (cm) | Length of Nail Visible After Hammering (cm) | Difference in Lengths (cm) |
|---|---|---|---|
| Nail with wedge | | | |
| Nail without wedge | | | |

Conclusion

Which nail was easier to hammer? Explain. _____

_____

_____

_____

# Unit 11: Screws
## Teacher Information

**Topic:** The screw represents an inclined plane wrapped around a cylinder.

**Standards:**
  **NSES** Unifying Concepts and Processes, (A), (B), (E), (F), (G)
  **NCTM** Numbers and Operations, Algebra, Geometry, and Measurement
  **STL** Technology and Society
  See **National Standards** section (pages 62–66) for more information on each standard.

**Concepts:**
- Two factors must be considered when measuring work: (1) the force applied and (2) the distance through which the force acts.
- Mechanical advantage compares the force produced by a machine with the force applied to the machine.

**Naïve Concepts:**
- Force is a property of an object.
- A machine is a device that uses an energy source such as electricity, gas, or coal to do work.

**Science Process Skills:**

Students will **make observations** about the relative force needed to move an object up slopes of varying degrees and **make inferences** about the mechanical advantage and the direction, force, and distance through which a force acts; **classify** tools into categories related to inclined planes, wedges, and screws; and **measure** the relative effort needed to move a resistance (load).

**Lesson Planner:**
1. <u>Directed Reading</u>: Introduce the concepts and essential vocabulary relating to screws using the directed reading exercise found on the Student Information page.
2. <u>Assessment</u>: Evaluate student comprehension of the information in the directed reading exercise using the quiz located on the Quick Check page.
3. <u>Concept Reinforcement</u>: Strengthen student understanding of concepts with the activities found on the Knowledge Builder page. **Materials Needed:** Activity #1—masking tape, screwdriver, marker, wood block, same size screws with different sized threads; Activity #2—paper towel tube, construction paper, pencil, marker

**Extension:** Students research the jackscrew and how it is used.

**Real World Application:** Screws can produce motion. The propeller of a boat and airplane are both screws. The propeller on a boat moves the craft through water while the airplane propeller moves the plane through the air.

# Unit 11: Screws
## Student Information

A screw is another simple machine. It is used to hold things together. A **screw** is an inclined plane wrapped around a cylinder or central point. In other words, it is a winding inclined plane. On screws, the line formed by the inclined plane is called a **thread**, or twisted inclined plane.

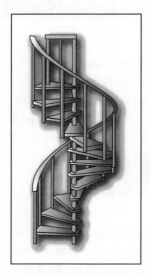

The **inclined plane** is a sloping, flat or plane surface over which objects may be rolled or lifted to higher elevations. As a staircase is an example of an inclined plane, the spiral staircase is an example of a screw. A screw achieves similar goals to an inclined plane in a smaller space. An example is the comparison of a conventional staircase to a spiral staircase. Both may achieve that same goal of providing access to a second floor; however, in the case of the spiral staircase, this is achieved with smaller floor space. Examples of inclined planes in the form of screws include the threads on drill bits, wood screw threads, bolts, spiral staircases, and augers.

As in the inclined plane, a screw is a simple machine that reduces the force required to move an object over a vertical distance or height. The distance between the threads is called the **pitch** of the screw. If a screw is represented by a bolt, then the effort is applied at one end by attaching a wrench and turning the bolt. Effort may also be applied to the handle of a screwdriver set in a groove in the head of a screw. As the effort force makes one complete circle, the head and axis of the bolt or screw make one complete turn, and the resistance force moves a distance equal to the pitch in the screw. Friction is a very important consideration when looking at the mechanical advantage of the screw.

pitch

**Ideal mechanical advantage (IMA)** for a screw is found by considering the following. If **r** is the length of the lever arm upon which effort force **(Fe)** acts, then, for one revolution, distance equals **2πr**, and the resistance moves the distance **d**, which is the pitch of the screw. **IMA = 2πr/d.**

A **compound machine** is two or more simple machines working together. The wood screw, drill bit, and auger are compound machines because the threads are inclined planes, but there is also a wedge on the points.

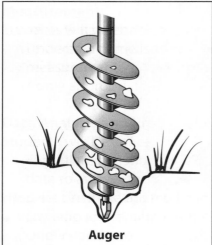

**Auger**

Name: _____   Date: _____

# Quick Check

## Matching

_____ 1.  inclined plane

_____ 2.  Fe

_____ 3.  screw

_____ 4.  pitch

_____ 5.  compound machine

a.  distance between the threads

b.  two or more simple machines working together

c.  effort force

d.  sloping, flat or plane surface over which objects may be rolled or lifted to higher elevations

e.  an inclined plane wrapped around a cylinder or central point, or a winding inclined plane

## Fill in the Blanks

6.  As a staircase is an example of an _____ _____, the spiral staircase is an example of a _____.

7.  On screws, the line formed by the inclined plane is called a _____.

8.  A screw achieves similar goals to an inclined plane in a smaller _____.

9.  The wood screw, drill bit, and auger are _____ _____ because the threads are inclined planes, but there is also a wedge on the points.

10. A screw is a simple machine that reduces the _____ required to move an object over a _____ distance or height.

## Multiple Choice

11. Which of the following is NOT an example of an inclined plane in the form of a screw?
    a.  auger
    b.  bolt
    c.  wood screw
    d.  knife

12. What kind of machine is a screw that does not have a point on the end?
    a.  compound machine
    b.  complex machine
    c.  simple machine
    d.  belt-driven machine

13. What is another name for the thread on a screw?
    a.  twisted inclined plane
    b.  wedge
    c.  spiral lever
    d.  inclined plane

Name: _____ Date: _____

# Knowledge Builder

## Activity #1: The Number of Turns

**Directions:** Place a wooden board and three screws of the same size but with different-sized threads on a table. Wrap a strip of masking tape around the handle of a screw driver. Make a vertical mark on the tape. Place the screw driver into the slot on the head of one screw. Watch where the mark is and start turning the screw to the right. Count one turn each time your mark comes back to the place it started. Count how many turns it takes to get the screw all the way into the wood. Record the number of turns in the chart below. Repeat for the other screws.

| Screws | Number of Turns |
|---|---|
| Screw #1 | |
| Screw #2 | |
| Screw #3 | |

Conclusion: Which type of screw took more turns to go into a block of wood? Why? _____

_____

## Activity #2: Screw Model

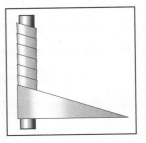

**Directions:** You will set up two models of the screw: one with a pencil as the core and one with a paper towel tube as the core. Measure the diameter of each cylinder core in centimeters. Then record the diameter and radius measurements in the data table below. Cut a rectangular sheet of paper diagonally into two right triangles. Use a marker to highlight the diagonal edge (hypotenuse) of your right triangle. Align the shorter leg of your right triangle to the side of your pencil, and wrap the paper triangle around the pencil. The highlighted hypotenuse of the paper triangle forms the thread of the screw. The paper inclined plane is wrapped around the cylinder. Record the pitch in centimeters in the data table below (the pitch is the distance between threads). Calculate the IMA. Then wrap the same paper triangle around the paper towel cylinder. Record the pitch in centimeters in the data table below, and calculate the IMA.

Example:    Dowel diameter = 2 cm      Dowel radius = 1 cm        $IMA = 2\pi r/d$
            Pitch of the screw = 3 cm   Distance (d) = Pitch        $IMA = 2 \times 3.14 \times 1 \text{ cm}/3 \text{ cm}$
                                                                    $IMA = 2.09$

| Cylinder | Diameter of Cylinder (cm) | Radius of Cylinder (cm) | Pitch of Screw (cm) | $IMA = 2\pi r/d$ |
|---|---|---|---|---|
| Pencil | | | | |
| Paper towel roll | | | | |

Conclusion: _____

_____

_____

Name: _____     Date: _____

# Inquiry Investigation Rubric

| Category | 4 | 3 | 2 | 1 |
|---|---|---|---|---|
| **Participation** | Used time well, cooperative, shared responsibilities, and focused on the task. | Participated, stayed focused on task most of the time. | Participated, but did not appear very interested. Focus was lost on several occasions. | Participation was minimal OR student was unable to focus on the task. |
| **Components of Investigation** | All required elements of the investigation were correctly completed and turned in on time. | All required elements were completed and turned in on time. | One required element was missing/or not completed correctly. | The work was turned in late and/or several required elements were missing and/or completed incorrectly. |
| **Procedure** | Steps listed in the procedure were accurately followed. | Steps listed in the procedure were followed. | Steps in the procedure were followed with some difficulty. | Unable to follow the steps in the procedure without assistance. |
| **Mechanics** | Flawless spelling, punctuation, and capitalization. | Few errors. | Careless or distracting errors. | Many errors. |

**Comments:**

# National Standards in Science, Math, and Technology

## *NSES Content Standards (NRC, 1996)*
National Research Council (1996). *National Science Education Standards.* Washington, D.C.: National Academy Press.

## UNIFYING CONCEPTS: K–12
**Systems, Order, and Organization:** The natural and designed world is complex. Scientists and students learn to define small portions for the convenience of investigation. The units of investigation can be referred to as systems. A system is an organized group of related objects or components that form a whole. Systems can consist of machines.

## Systems, Order, and Organization
The goal of this standard is to ...
- Think and analyze in terms of systems.
- Assume that the behavior of the universe is not capricious. Nature is predictable.
- Understand the regularities in a system.
- Understand that prediction is the use of knowledge to identify and explain observations.
- Understand that the behavior of matter, objects, organisms, or events has order and can be described statistically.

## Evidence, Models, and Explanation
The goal of this standard is to ...
- Recognize that evidence consists of observations and data on which to base scientific explanations.
- Recognize that models have explanatory power.
- Recognize that scientific explanations incorporate existing scientific knowledge (laws, principles, theories, paradigms, models), and new evidence from observations, experiments, or models.
- Recognize that scientific explanations should reflect a rich scientific knowledge base, evidence of logic, higher levels of analysis, greater tolerance of criticism and uncertainty, and a clear demonstration of the relationship between logic, evidence, and current knowledge.

## Change, Constancy, and Measurement
The goal of this standard is to …
- Recognize that some properties of objects are characterized by constancy, including the speed of light, the charge of an electron, and the total mass plus energy of the universe.
- Recognize that changes might occur in the properties of materials, position of objects, motion, and form and function of systems.
- Recognize that changes in systems can be quantified.
- Recognize that measurement systems may be used to clarify observations.

# National Standards in Science, Math, and Technology (cont.)

## Form and Function

The goal of this standard is to …

- Recognize that the form of an object is frequently related to its use, operation, or function.
- Recognize that function frequently relies on form.
- Recognize that form and function apply to different levels of organization.
- Enable students to explain function by referring to form, and explain form by referring to function.

## NSES Content Standard A: Inquiry

- Abilities necessary to do scientific inquiry
  - Identify questions that can be answered through scientific investigations.
  - Design and conduct a scientific investigation.
  - Use appropriate tools and techniques to gather, analyze, and interpret data.
  - Develop descriptions, explanations, predictions, and models using evidence.
  - Think critically and logically to make relationships between evidence and explanations.
  - Recognize and analyze alternative explanations and predictions.
  - Communicate scientific procedures and explanations.
  - Use mathematics in all aspects of scientific inquiry.
- Understanding about inquiry
  - Different kinds of questions suggest different kinds of scientific investigations.
  - Current scientific knowledge and understanding guide scientific investigations.
  - Mathematics is important in all aspects of scientific inquiry.
  - Technology used to gather data enhances accuracy and allows scientists to analyze and quantify results of investigations.
  - Scientific explanations emphasize evidence, have logically consistent arguments, and use scientific principles, models, and theories.
  - Science advances through legitimate skepticism.
  - Scientific investigations sometimes result in new ideas and phenomena for study, generate new methods or procedures, or develop new technologies to improve data collection.

## NSES Content Standard B: Physical Science (Transfer of Energy) 5–8

- Energy is a property of many substances and is associated with heat, light, electricity, mechanical motion, sound, nuclei, and the nature of a chemical; energy is transferred in many ways.
- Electrical circuits provide a means of transferring electrical energy when heat, light, sound, or chemical changes are produced.
- In most chemical and nuclear reactions, energy is transferred into or out of a system. Heat, light, mechanical motion, or electricity might all be involved in such transfers.

# National Standards in Science, Math, and Technology (cont.)

## NSES Content Standard E: Science and Technology 5–8

• Abilities of technological design
  * Identify appropriate problems for technological design.
  * Design a solution or product.
  * Implement the proposed design.
  * Evaluate completed technological designs or products.
  * Communicate the process of technological design.
• Understanding about science and technology
  * Scientific inquiry and technological design have similarities and differences.
  * Many people in different cultures have made and continue to make contributions.
  * Science and technology are reciprocal.
  * Perfectly designed solutions do not exist.
  * Technological designs have constraints.
  * Technological solutions have intended benefits and unintended consequences.

## NSES Content Standard F: Science in Personal and Social Perspectives 5–8

• Science and technology in society
  * Science influences society through its knowledge and world view.
  * Societal challenges often inspire questions for scientific research.
  * Technology influences society through its products and processes.
  * Scientists and engineers work in many different settings.
  * Science cannot answer all questions, and technology cannot solve all human problems.

## NSES Content Standard G: History and Nature of Science 5–8

• Science as human endeavor
• Nature of science
  * Scientists formulate and test their explanations of nature using observation, experiments, and theoretical and mathematical models.
  * It is normal for scientists to differ with one another about interpretation of evidence and theory.
  * It is part of scientific inquiry for scientists to evaluate the results of other scientists' work.
• History of science
  * Many individuals have contributed to the traditions of science.
  * Science has been and is practiced by different individuals in different cultures.
  * Tracing the history of science can show how difficult it was for scientific innovators to break through the accepted ideas of their time to reach the conclusions we now accept.

# National Standards in Science, Math, and Technology (cont.)

**Standards for Technological Literacy (STL) ITEA, 2000**
International Technology Education Association (2000). *Standards for Technological Literacy.* Reston, VA: International Technology Education Association.

## The Nature of Technology
Students will develop an understanding of the:
1.  Characteristics and scope of technology.
2.  Core concepts of technology.
3.  Relationships among technologies and the connections between technology and other fields of study.

## Technology and Society
Students will develop an understanding of the:
4.  Cultural, social, economic, and political effects of technology.
5.  Effects of technology on the environment.
6.  Role of society in the development and use of technology.
7.  Influence of technology on history.

## Design
Students will develop an understanding of the:
8.  Attributes of design.
9.  Engineering design.
10. Role of troubleshooting, research and development, invention and innovation, and experimentation in problem solving.

## Abilities for a Technological World
Students will develop abilities to:
11. Apply the design process.
12. Use and maintain technological products and systems.
13. Assess the impact of products and systems.

## The Designed World
Students will develop an understanding of and be able to select and use:
14. Medical technologies.
15. Agricultural and related biotechnologies.
16. Energy and power technologies.
17. Information and communication technologies.
18. Transportation technologies.
19. Manufacturing technologies.
20. Construction technologies.

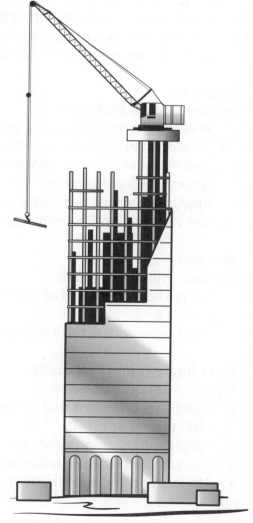

# National Standards in Science, Math, and Technology (cont.)

## *Principles and Standards for School Mathematics (NCTM), 2000*

National Council for Teachers of Mathematics (2000). *Principles and Standards for School Mathematics.* Reston, VA: National Council for Teachers of Mathematics.

### Number and Operations

Students will be enabled to:

- Understand numbers, ways of representing numbers, relationships among numbers, and number systems.
- Understand meanings of operations and how they relate to one another.
- Compute fluently and make reasonable estimates.

### Algebra

Students will be enabled to:

- Understand patterns, relations, and functions.
- Represent and analyze mathematical situations and structures using algebraic symbols.
- Use mathematical models to represent and understand quantitative relationships.
- Analyze change in various contexts.

### Geometry

Students will be enabled to:

- Analyze characteristics and properties of two- and three-dimensional geometric shapes and develop mathematical arguments about geometric relationships.
- Specify locations and describe spatial relationships using coordinate geometry and other representational systems.
- Apply transformations and use symmetry to analyze mathematical situations.
- Use visualization, spatial reasoning, and geometric modeling to solve problems.

### Measurement

Students will be enabled to:

- Understand measurable attributes of objects and the units, systems, and processes of measurement.
- Apply appropriate techniques, tools, and formulas to determine measurements.

### Data Analysis and Probability

Students will be enabled to:

- Formulate questions that can be addressed with data and collect, organize, and display relevant data to answer them.
- Select and use appropriate statistical methods to analyze data.
- Develop and evaluate inferences and predictions that are based on data.
- Understand and apply basic concepts of probability.

# Science Process Skills

**Introduction:** Science is organized curiosity, and an important part of this organization includes the thinking skills or information-processing skills. We ask the question "why?" and then must plan a strategy for answering the question or questions. In the process of answering our questions, we make and carefully record observations, make predictions, identify and control variables, measure, make inferences, and communicate our findings. Additional skills may be called upon, depending on the nature of our questions. In this way, science is a verb, involving active manipulation of materials and careful thinking. Science is dependent on language, math, and reading skills, as well as the specialized thinking skills associated with identifying and solving problems.

## BASIC PROCESS SKILLS:

**Classifying:** Grouping, ordering, arranging, or distributing objects, events, or information into categories based on properties or criteria, according to some method or system.

> *Example:* The skill is being demonstrated if the student is placing a set of hand tools and kitchen utensils into simple machine categories.

**Observing:** Using the senses (or extensions of the senses) to gather information about an object or event.

> *Example:* The skill is being demonstrated if the student is seeing and describing the setup of the three classes of levers, noting the differences between them.

**Measuring:** Using both standard and nonstandard measures or estimates to describe the dimensions of an object or event. Making quantitative observations.

> *Example:* The skill is being demonstrated if the student is using a Newton scale to measure the force needed to move an object up an inclined plane.

**Inferring:** Making an interpretation or conclusion based on reasoning to explain an observation.

> *Example:* The skill is being demonstrated if the student is stating that the effort required to move a resistance in a first-class lever is related to the relative distance of the effort and resistance from the fulcrum.

**Communicating:** Communicating ideas through speaking or writing. Students may share the results of investigations, collaborate on solving problems, and gather and interpret data both orally and in writing. Using graphs, charts, and diagrams to describe data.

> *Example:* The skill is being demonstrated if the student is describing an event or a set of observations; summarizing data, interpreting findings, and offering conclusions; or using a graph to show the relationship between distance and the effort in a first-class lever.

# Science Process Skills (cont.)

**Predicting:** Making a forecast of future events or conditions in the context of previous observations and experiences.

> *Example:* The skill is being demonstrated if the student is predicting the effects of the distance of an object from a fulcrum and the resulting effort needed to move the object.

**Manipulating Materials:** Handling or treating materials and equipment skillfully and effectively.

> *Example:* The skill is being demonstrated if the student is setting up three inclined planes with varying slopes and measuring and comparing the force needed to move an object up each of the inclined planes.

**Replicating:** Performing acts that duplicate demonstrated symbols, patterns, or procedures.

> *Example:* The skill is being demonstrated if the student is operating a Newton spring scale following procedures previously demonstrated or modeled by another person.

**Using Numbers:** Applying mathematical rules or formulas to calculate quantities or determine relationships from basic measurements.

> *Example:* The skill is being demonstrated if the student is computing the ideal mechanical advantage for a first-class lever system.

**Developing Vocabulary:** Specialized terminology and unique uses of common words in relation to a given topic need to be identified and given meaning.

> *Example:* Using context clues, working definitions, glossaries or dictionaries, word structure (roots, prefixes, suffixes), and synonyms and antonyms to clarify meaning, i.e., effort force, resistance force, load, ideal mechanical advantage, pitch.

**Questioning:** Questions serve to focus inquiry, determine prior knowledge, and establish purposes or expectations for an investigation. An active search for information is promoted when questions are used.

> *Example:* The skill is being demonstrated if the student is using what is already known about a topic or concept to formulate questions for further investigation.

**Using Clues:** Key words and symbols convey significant meaning in messages. Organizational patterns facilitate comprehension of major ideas. Graphic features clarify textual information.

> *Example:* Listing or underlining words and phrases that carry the most important details, or relating key words together to express a main idea or concept.

# Science Process Skills (cont.)

**INTEGRATED PROCESS SKILLS**

**Creating Models:** Displaying information by means of graphic illustrations or other multisensory representations.

> *Example:* The skill is being demonstrated if the student is drawing a graph or diagram or constructing a three-dimensional object that illustrates information about the setup of a simple or compound machine.

**Formulating Hypotheses:** Stating or constructing a statement that is testable about what is thought to be the expected outcome of an experiment (based on reasoning).

> *Example:* The skill is being demonstrated if the student is making a statement to be used as the basis for an experiment: "If the mass is increased in a first-class lever, then the effort will increase proportionately."

**Generalizing:** Drawing general conclusions from particulars.

> *Example:* The skill is being demonstrated if the student is making a summary statement following analysis of experimental results.

**Identifying and Controlling Variables:** Recognizing the characteristics of objects or factors in events that are constant or change under different conditions and that can affect an experimental outcome, keeping most variables constant while manipulating only one variable.

> *Example:* The skill is being demonstrated if the student is listing or describing the factors that are thought to, or would, influence the amount of effort needed to lift a mass using a first-class lever.

**Defining Operationally:** Stating how to measure a variable in an experiment; defining a variable according to the actions or operations to be performed on or with it.

> *Example:* The skill is being demonstrated if the student is defining such things as resistance in the context of the materials and actions for a specific activity. Hence, resistance may be represented by the number of washers loaded on one end of a lever.

# Science Process Skills (cont.)

**Recording and Interpreting Data:** Collecting bits of information about objects and events that illustrate a specific situation, organizing and analyzing data that has been obtained, and drawing conclusions from it by determining apparent patterns or relationships in the data.

> *Example:* The skill is being demonstrated if the student is recording data (taking notes, making lists/outlines, recording numbers on charts/graphs, making tape recordings, taking photographs, writing numbers of results of observations/measurements).

**Making Decisions:** Identifying alternatives and choosing a course of action from among alternatives after basing the judgment for the selection on justifiable reasons.

> *Example:* The skill is being demonstrated if the student is identifying alternative ways to solve a problem through the utilization of a simple or compound machine; analyzing the consequences of each alternative, such as cost and the effect on other people or the environment; using justifiable reasons as the basis for making choices; and choosing freely from the alternatives.

**Experimenting:** Being able to conduct an experiment, including asking an appropriate question, stating a hypothesis, identifying and controlling variables, operationally defining those variables, designing a "fair" experiment, and interpreting the results of an experiment.

> *Example:* The skill is being demonstrated if the student is utilizing the entire process of designing, building, and testing various simple or compound machines to solve a problem.

# Definitions of Terms

**Acceleration** equals net force/mass.

**Actual Mechanical Advantage** is the ratio of the resistance force to the effort force.

**Advantage** is related to resistance and force. The ratio of the resistance force to the effort force is called ideal mechanical advantage.

The **Archimedian screw** was a device invented to raise water.

A **belt system** is a compound machine made up of the wheel and axle and pulley.

In a **block and tackle system**, pulleys can change the direction of a force and multiply the force. The block and tackle system consists of a fixed and a movable pulley.

A **bolt** or screw is an inclined plane wrapped around a central point, or a winding inclined plane.

A **cantilever** is an example of a lever that consists of a bar supported at only one end.

The **catapult** is a machine that works like a slingshot and is capable of launching heavy objects.

When two or more simple machines work together to perform one task, it becomes a **compound machine**.

A belt looped around two pulleys in a **crossed pattern arrangement** will cause the wheels to rotate in opposite directions.

The gear on which the force is applied is the driver, and the other gear is the **driven gear**.

The gear on which the force is applied is the **driver**, and the other gear is the driven gear.

**Effort** is represented by the force that you apply to move a load (resistance). Effort is sometimes referred to as **effort force**.

**Energy** is the ability to do work.

Using a **first-class lever**, the force changes directions. The load is on one side of the fulcrum, and the forces are on the other side of the lever.

A **force** is any push or pull in a particular direction or that which produces or prevents motion.

**Friction** is a force that resists motion.

A **fulcrum** or pivot point is a fixed point.

Two or more gears meshed together are called a **gear train**.

**Gear wheel** combinations of different diameters are used to increase or decrease speed.

**Gears** are toothed wheels and axles.

**Ideal Mechanical Advantage (IMA)** is the ratio of the distance the effort force moves to the distance the resistance force moves.

# Definitions of Terms (cont.)

Any gears between the driver and the driven gear are called **idlers**.

The **inclined plane** is a device that allows us to increase the height of an object without lifting it vertically.

Between the eighteenth and nineteenth centuries, the **Industrial Revolution** began in Europe and spread to North America. Factories using power-driven compound machines quickly replaced the old method of handmade goods.

**Kinetic energy** is energy due to the motion of a mass.

The **Law of Acceleration**, Newton's Second Law of Motion, states that acceleration produced by a force on a body is directly proportional to the magnitude of the net force, is in the same direction as the force, and is inversely proportional to the mass of the body.

The **Law of Action and Reaction**, Newton's Third Law of Motion, states that for every action there is an equal and opposite reaction.

The **Law of Inertia**, Newton's First Law of Motion, states an object at rest stays at rest until acted upon by another force; it stays in motion in a straight line at a constant speed until acted upon by another force.

Isaac Newton's three **Laws of Motion** include the Laws of Inertia, Acceleration, and Action and Reaction.

A **lever** is a rigid bar that is free to rotate about a point called a fulcrum.

The resistance or **load** is the object being moved.

A **machine** is any device that makes doing work easier.

The measure of the quantity of matter that a body contains is called **mass**.

**Mechanical advantage** compares the force produced by a machine with the force applied to the machine. It can be found by dividing the force of resistance by the force of the effort.

**Motion** is the act of moving from one place to another.

A **movable pulley** is set up so the force and load move in the same direction. A movable pulley resembles a second-class lever. The fulcrum is at the end of the lever where the supporting rope touches the pulley.

In the metric system, force is measured in **newton**s. A newton is used because it includes both mass and acceleration of mass. Note that acceleration includes distance and time, or rate of change of velocity. Force then equals mass times acceleration. One kilogram meter/sec$^2$.

The belt looped around two pulleys in a **parallel arrangement** will cause both wheels to rotate in the same direction.

The distance between the threads is called the **pitch** of the screw.

# Definitions of Terms (cont.)

A fulcrum or **pivot point** is a fixed point.

**Potential energy** is stored energy or energy due to the position of a mass.

**Power** is the time rate of doing work or the rate of doing work. Hence, power equals work divided by time or P = W / t.

The **pulley** is a wheel that turns readily on an axle. The axle is usually mounted on a frame.

A **ramp** spreads the force over a longer distance, so it takes less force to lift an object.

The **relative size** of the pulleys in a belt system will determine the mechanical advantage.

The **resistance** or load is the object being moved.

The **resistance force** referred to in this book is the force of gravity.

In a **second-class lever**, the load is placed between the force and the fulcrum. The direction of the force stays the same as the load.

The **screw** is an inclined plane wound around a cylinder.

A **simple belt system** consists of two pulley wheels and a belt.

**Simple machines** change the amount, distance, or direction of a force needed to do work.

A **single fixed pulley** behaves like a first-class lever with the fulcrum (axis of the pulley) between the force and the load. The load moves up as the force goes down. This type of pulley only changes the direction of the force.

The **third-class lever** is similar to the first-class lever with the fulcrum at one end and the load on the other end. However, a third-class lever has the force applied between the fulcrum and the load.

On screws, the line formed by the inclined plane is called a **thread**, or twisted inclined plane.

**Torque** is a moment of force that causes a rotation. Moment of force refers to mass times distance. Levers, pulleys, and the wheel and axle all involve torque.

The **wedge** is a double inclined plane.

The measure of the attractive force of the earth for a body is called the **weight** of the body.

The **wheel and axle** is a wheel rigidly fixed to an axle.

A **winch system** is an example of a wheel and axle. The wheel portion of the system is represented by a crank, and the axle is represented by the cylinder-shaped body.

**Work** is the force needed to move an object though a distance.

# Answer Keys

## Historical Perspective
### Quick Check (page 6)
*Matching*
1. e    2. d    3. b    4. a    5. c

*Fill in the Blank*
6. Industrial Revolution    7. Archimedes
8. action, reaction    9. force, net force
10. motion, constant

*Multiple Choice*
11. b    12. c    13. c

## Machines
### Quick Check (page 10)
*Matching*
1. b    2. e    3. a    4. c    5. d

*Fill in the Blank*
6. levers, inclined planes    7. machine
8. Compound machines    9. complex
10. inclined plane

*Multiple Choice*
11. d    12. b    13. d

### Knowledge Builder (page 11)
*Activity #2*
1. The wheel and axle holds the (wedge) cutter on. The lever is the handle. The wedge cuts the can as the wheel turns and moves the opener around the can lid.

## Force and Motion
### Quick Check (page 14)
*Matching*
1. d    2. e    3. c    4. b    5. a

*Fill in the Blank*
6. Mechanical advantage    7. Mechanical energy
8. force, motion    9. Kinetic energy
10. force, distance

*Multiple Choice*
11. a    12. d    13. b

### Knowledge Builder (page 15)
*Activity #1*
1. heat
2. No, the soap made the surface of the hands slippery and reduced friction.

*Conclusion:*
1. The soap acted as a lubricant.
2. Oil is a lubricant; lubricants reduce friction and keep parts from wearing out.

*Activity #2*
1. (+), check, check    2. (–), check, no check
3. (–), check, no check    4. (+), check, check

## Levers
### Quick Check (page 18)
*Matching*
1. c    2. d    3. b    4. e    5. a

*Fill in the Blank*
6. force, direction    7. resistance    8. second
9. third    10. first

*Multiple Choice*
11. a    12. b    13. c

### Knowledge Builder (pages 19–22)
*Activity #1*
1. The distance between the fulcrum and the resistance decreased as more mass was added to the cup.
2. The direction of the force was down.
3. The resistance went up.

*Conclusion:* A first-class lever multiplies the force and changes the direction of the force.

*Activity #2*
1. The length of the rubber band decreased as the fulcrum was moved closer to the cup.
2. The direction of the force was down.
3. The resistance went up.

*Conclusion:* A first-class lever multiplies the force and changes the direction of the force.

*Activity #3*
1. As the resistance was moved closer to the fulcrum, the force needed to lift the resistance decreased.
2. The direction of the force was up.
3. The direction the resistance was moving was up.

*Conclusion:* The second-class lever multiplies the force.

*Activity #4*
1. As the force was moved closer to the resistance, the force needed to lift the resistance decreased.
2. The direction of the force was up.
3. The direction the resistance was moving was up.

*Conclusion:* Answers may vary but should include a third-class lever has the force applied between the fulcrum and the resistance. The force and the resistance are moving in the same direction. Third-class levers multiply the force but do not change the direction of the force.

### Inquiry Investigation (page 23)
*Conclusion:* First-class lever. In the first-class lever and the cantilever, the force changes directions, the load is on one side of the fulcrum, and the forces are on the other side of the fulcrum. When the force pushes down on one end, the load moves up.

## Wheels and Axles
### Quick Check (page 27)
*Matching*

1. d   2. c   3. e   4. a   5. b

*Fill in the Blank*

6. shaft       7. simple   8. mechanical advantage
9. wheel, axle   10. lever

*Multiple Choice*

11. c   12. c   13. c

### Knowledge Builder (page 28)

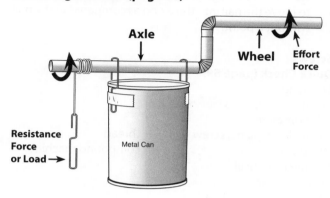

## Pulleys
### Quick Check (page 31)
*Matching*

1. c   2. e   3. d   4. b   5. a

*Fill in the Blank*

6. Pulleys          7. force, movement
8. downward, up   9. force, motion   10. fulcrum

*Multiple Choice*

11. a   12. d   13. a

### Knowledge Builder (page 32–34)

*Activity #1*

1. There was little or no difference in the length of the rubber band.
2. The amount of force needed to lift the cup and the pennies was the same.
3. Only the direction of the load versus the effort force was changed.

*Activity #2*

1. There was a difference in the length of the rubber band.
2. The amount of force needed to lift the cup and pennies was changed using the movable pulley.
3. The direction of the load and effort force were the same.

*Activity #3*

1. There was a difference in the length of the rubber band.
2. The amount of force needed to lift the cup and pennies changed using the block and tackle pulley system.
3. The direction of the resistance movement and effort movement were different.

## Gears
### Quick Check (page 38)
*Matching*

1. c   2. e   3. d   4. a   5. b

*Fill in the Blank*

6. Gears                    7. rotations
8. power, rotation, speed   9. increase, decrease
10. compound machine

*Multiple Choice*

11. b   12. c   13. d

### Knowledge Builder (pages 39–40)

*Activity #1*

Answers will vary depending on the number of gear teeth and wheel diameter.

*Activity #2*

Test #1: low gear

Test #2: high gear; Lower gears make the pedals easy to turn, pedaling faster than your ideal cadence can allow you to generate an extra burst of speed.

Test #3: high gear; low gear

Test #4: yes; yes; middle

## Belt Systems
### Quick Check (page 43)
*Matching*

1. a   2. d   3. e   4. c   5. b

*Fill in the Blank*

6. parallel          7. crossed       8. friction
9. wheel, axle, simple   10. energy, second

*Multiple Choice*

11. b   12. b   13. b

### Knowledge Builder (pages 44–45)

A. See chart completed as an example.
B. Description: Two wheels of equal diameter with a cross pattern belt setup
   Sketch:

   Predict: Answers will vary.
   Observed: Second spool will turn in the opposite direction as the first spool and at the same speed.
C. Description: Four wheels of equal diameter with parallel belt setup
   Sketch:

   Predict: Answers will vary.
   Observed: Spools all turn in the same direction and at the same speed.
D. Description: Four wheels of equal diameter with parallel belt setup and cross pattern belt setup
   Sketch:

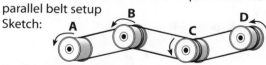

Predict: Answers will vary.

Observed: Spools will turn in different directions and at the same speed.

E. Description: Two wheels of equal diameter and one smaller wheel; parallel belt setup

Sketch:

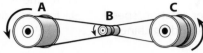

Predict: Answers will vary.

Observed: Spools will turn in the same direction, but the smaller spool will turn faster.

## Inclined Planes
### Quick Check (page 48)
*Matching*

1. a    2. d    3. b    4. e    5. c

*Fill in the Blank*

6. simple machine    7. ramp    8. gravity
9. wedge    10. compound machines

*Multiple Choice*

11. c    12. d    13. a

### Knowledge Builder (page 49)
*Activity #1*

The longer and more gradual the slope of the inclined plane, the less force is needed to move an object up the slope. As the slope decreases, the friction increases between the object being moved up the slope and the surface of the inclined plane.

*Activity #2*

The longer the inclined plane is compared to its height, the greater its mechanical advantage.

### Inquiry Investigation (pages 50–51)

*Hypothesis:* Mass does/does not affect the speed of a toy car rolling down a ramp.

*Conclusion:* Answers will vary but should include the following information: The purpose, a brief description of the procedure, and whether or not the hypothesis was supported by the data collected. (The greater the mass of an object, the greater the speed due to inertia.)

## Wedges
### Quick Check (page 54)
*Matching*

1. c    2. a    3. b    4. e    5. d

*Fill in the Blank*

6. inclined plane    7. differences    8. resistance
9. parallel, vertical    10. opening, wedges

*Multiple Choice*

11. c    12. d    13. c

### Knowledge Builder (pages 55–56)
*Activity #1*

*Conclusion:* The longer and thinner the wedge, the greater the mechanical advantage. The wedge with the longest incline relative to its width at the thickest part will require the least force to separate or split an object.

*Activity #2*

*Conclusion:* The nail with a point. The point on the nail is a wedge. The wedge allows a person to exert less force to move the nail into the wood as compared to the nail without a point.

## Screws
### Quick Check (page 59)
*Matching*

1. d    2. c    3. e    4. a    5. b

*Fill in the Blank*

6. inclined plane, screw    7. thread
8. space    9. compound machines
10. force, vertical

*Multiple Choice*

11. d    12. c    13. a

### Knowledge Builder (page 60)
*Activity #1*

*Conclusion:* The screw with the smaller pitch took more turns. The smaller the pitch of a screw, the greater its mechanical advantage, which means it is easier to turn. However, it takes longer to screw into the wood.

*Activity #2*

*Conclusion:* Answers may vary but should include: The screw with the smaller core radius produces the threads that are closer together. The smaller pitch means a greater mechanical advantage, which means it is easier to move the load up the incline.

# Bibliography

## Student Literature Resources:

Alexander, R. McNeil. *Exploring Biomechanics: Animals in Motion*. New York: Scientific American Library. 1992.

Blackburn, Ken and Jeff Lammers. *The World Record Paper Airplane Book*. New York: Workman Publishing. 2006.

Eichelberger, Barbara and Connie Larson. *Constructions for Children: Projects in Design Technology*. Palo Alto, CA: Dale Seymour Publications. 1993.

Glover, David. *Make It Work: Machines*. New York: Scholastic. 1994.

Gunderson, P. Erik. *The Handy Physics Answer Book*. Detroit: Visible Ink Press. 1998.

Kalman, Bobbie. *Historic Communities: Tools and Gadgets*. New York: Crabtree Publishing Co. 1992.

Lafferty, Peter. *Force and Motion: Eyewitness Science*. New York: Dorling Kindersley. 1992.

Lorenz, Albert. *Metropolis: Ten Cities Ten Centuries*. New York: Harry N. Abrams, Inc. 1996.

Macaulay, David. *The New Way Things Work*. Boston: Houghton Mifflin Company. 1998.

Macaulay, David. *Building Big*. Boston: Houghton Mifflin Company. 2004.

Marson, Ron. *Machines*. Canby, OH: Tops Learning Systems. 1989.

Nankivell-Aston, Sally and Dorothy Jackson. *Science Experiments with Forces*. Danbury, CT: Children's Press. 2000.

Nankivell-Aston, Sally and Dorothy Jackson. *Science Experiments with Simple Machines*. New York: Franklin Watts. 2000.

National Science Resources Center. *Energy, Machines, and Motion*. Burlington, NC: Carolina Biological Supply Company. 2007.

Reid, Struan and Patricia Fara. *The Usborne Book of Discovery*. Tulsa, OK: EDC Publishing. 1994.

Richards, Jon. *Science Factory: Work & Simple Machines*. Mankato, MN: Stargazer Books. 2004.

Rogers, Kristeen. *The Usborne Science Encyclopedia*. London: Usborne Publishing Ltd. 2009.

St. Andre, Ralph. *Simple Machines Made Simple*. Engelwood, CO: Teacher Ideas Press. 1993.

Stanish, Bob and Carol Singletary. *Inventioneering: Nurturing Intellectual Talent in the Classroom*. Carthage, IL: Good Apple, Inc. 1987.

Taylor, Beverly, Dwight Portman, and Susan Gertz. *Teaching Physics with Toys*. Middletown, OH: Terrific Science Press. 2006.

Thorne-Thomsen, Kathleen. *Frank Lloyd Wright for Kids*. Chicago: Chicago Press Review. 1994.

Williams, Trevor. *The History of Invention: From Stone Axes to Silicon Chips*. New York: Checkmark Books. 2000.

Young, Jay. *Beyond Amazing: Six Spectacular Science Pop-ups*. New York: HarperCollins. 1997.

# Bibliography (cont.)

## Software:

Asimov, Issac. *The Ultimate Robot*. Byron Press Multimedia Company, Inc. 1993.

*Widget Workshop*. Oranda, CA: Maxis, Inc. 1995.

*Car Builder*. Hilton Head, SC: Optimum Resource, Inc. 1997.

*Encyclopedia of Science*. New York, NY: Dorling Kindersley Multimedia. 1995.

*Inventor Labs: Technology*. Pleasantville, NY: Houghton Mifflin interactive. 1997.

*Inventor Labs: Transportation*. Pleasantville, NY: Houghton Mifflin interactive. 1997.

Kelly, Robin. *Gizmos & Gadgets!* Minneapolis, MN: The Learning Company. 1994.

Macaulay, David. *The New Way Things Work*. New York: Dorling Kindersley Interactive Learning. 1994.

## Web Resources:

http://phys.udallas.edu

http://www.physics.montana.edu/physed/misconceptions

http://www.exploratorium.edu/cycling/

www.pbs.org/wgbh/nova/lostempires/obelisk/

www.mos.org/Leonardo

www.howstuffworks.com/gears.htm

www.howstuffworks.com/pulley.htm

www.howstuffworks.com/tower-crane.htm

## Curriculum Resources:

Erickson, Sheldon. *Brick Layers II, AIMS Activities Grades 4–9*. Fresno, CA: AIMS Education Foundation. 2000.

Hewitt, Paul. *Conceptual Physics: High School 10th Edition*. Menlo Park, CA: Addison Wesley Longman. 2008.

Hewitt, Paul, John Suchocki, and Leslie Hewitt. *Conceptual Physical Science, 4th Edition*. Menlo Park, CA: Addison Wesley Longman. 2007.

Lorbeer, George. *Science Activities for Middle-School Students*. Boston: McGraw Hill. 2000.

Taylor, Beverly, Dwight Portman, and Susan Gertz. *Teaching Physics with Toys*. Middletown, OH: Terrific Science Press. 2006.

Taylor, Bob. *Teaching Energy with Toys: Complete Lessons for Grades 4–8*. Middletown, OH: Terrific Science Press. 1998.